# ON THE COBBLES

# ON THE COBBLES

## THE LIFE OF A BARE-KNUCKLE GYPSY WARRIOR

**JIMMY STOCKINS**
**with Martin King and Martin Knight**

EDINBURGH AND LONDON

**This book is dedicated to**
**my father, Muggy Stockins,**
**a man who loved life.**
**Keep smiling, Dad.**



First published in Great Britain in 2000 by
MAINSTREAM PUBLISHING COMPANY (EDINBURGH) LTD
7 Albany Street
Edinburgh EH1 3UG

This edition 2001
Reprinted 2002, 2004

ISBN 1 84018 509 0



A catalogue record for this book is available from the British Library

Typeset in Opti Looking Glass and Van Djick
Printed and bound in Great Britain by Cox & Wyman Ltd

# CONTENTS

# PREFACE

Anyone who knows me knows I didn't write this book. Because I don't read or write, so I couldn't have done, could I? Notice I say *don't* read or write not *can't* read or write. Many gypsies choose not to learn to read and write, or their parents choose for them. It's a way of keeping the outside world out, I suppose. Some people take this to mean that we are stupid, but that's normally a big mistake. Think about it for a minute – could you live off your wits, the land and on the streets if you were basically stupid? Of course not.

However, this book *is* my story. My words. The two Martins have put them in the right order for me, encouraged me to remember people, incidents and times. They've put it all together from hour on hour of conversations with me, my family and my friends. Every bit has been read back to me, until I'm happy that's the way it was, the best I can remember it. I hope the book gives respect to all the gypsy warriors and the many other people – travellers and gorgers alike – who have made my life what it was and is. At the same time, I hope that *On the Cobbles* gives an insight into the sport of bare-knuckle fighting and a glimpse of what being a gypsy in the 21st century is all about.

**Jimmy**
**August 2000**

# GLOSSARY

The following list of Romany words, with their common English equivalents, is not intended to be comprehensive. Jimmy and his friends use a mixture of slang, cockney and Romany in their everyday speech, and below are the more frequently used, but possibly unfamiliar, terms.

| ROMANY | ENGLISH |
|---|---|
| Banged up | In prison |
| Bird | Prison sentence |
| Bory | Big/pregnant |
| Brimson | A bullshitter/someone living in a fantasy world |
| Brogues | Trousers |
| Cadie | Hat |
| Canny | Bird/pheasant |
| Cans | Money |
| Chavvy | Child/baby |
| Chicken fighting | Cockfighting |
| Chokkas | Shoes |
| Chore/chorin | Steal/stealing |

| | |
|---|---|
| Chuck | Food |
| Claret | Blood |
| Coeey | Rat |
| Coover | A utility noun, e.g. used to describe a thing, an object |
| Corr | A fight |
| Cory | Penis |
| Crack | Wood |
| Cushty | Good/fine |
| Dell | Hit |
| Dimelow/Dinelow | Idiot/fool |
| Dordy | Oh dear! |
| Dosh | Money |
| Drag | Car |
| Fams | Hands |
| Faumy | Ring |
| Flush | Holding money/cash |
| Garlo | Policeman |
| Gatter | Drink/alcohol |
| Gavvers | The police |
| Gilly | Man |
| Gorger/gorgia | Non-gypsy or traveller/everyone else |
| Gry | Horse |
| Hatchintan | Gypsy site |
| Headinams | Spinning-the-coin game |
| Hedge Mumper | Tramp |
| Hummel | Hair |
| Jell/let's jell | Get away/scarper |
| Jethro | Coat |
| Jigger | Door |
| Joey Grey | Rabbit stew |
| Jug | Bank |
| Juice | Petrol |
| Juk | Dog |

| | |
|---|---|
| Jumping the broomstick | Eloping |
| Kenna | House |
| Kennec | Non-gypsy or traveller/everyone else |
| Ker | Do |
| Kitchema | Pub/club |
| Long-tail | Rat |
| Loud/get loud | To be arrested |
| Mandy | Myself |
| Mitcham gypsy | Not a true gypsy |
| Mooey | Mouth |
| Mulady | Devil/ghost |
| Mullered | Dead |
| Munging | Selling lucky heather |
| Musgro | Policeman |
| Mush | Fella/bloke |
| Needies | Gypsy |
| Old Bill | Police |
| Parni | Water |
| Peeve | Drink/alcohol |
| Pikey | Term for traveller, used mainly by gorgers |
| Pooker | Signpost |
| Poov | Grass |
| Poov the gry | Graze the horse |
| Puff | Marijuana/dope |
| Purr | Stomach/belly |
| Rakli | Girl/lady |
| Rocker | Speak the language |
| Rooker | Tree |
| Rumored | Married |
| Says | Stories/tales |
| Score | Buy/purchase |
| Scran | Food |
| Sheero | Head |

| | |
|---|---|
| Showmen | The travelling fairground families and community, also known by gypsies as bread-and-jam eaters or penny-pinchers |
| Shushi | Rabbit |
| Site | Gypsy encampment, permanent or temporary |
| Skimaged | Drunk |
| Spark/sparked | Knocked out |
| Spinner/sulky | Tin box attached to a horse. Where the rider sits when racing in a trotting match |
| Straightener | A fair fight |
| Switch off | To knock unconscious |
| Toby | Footpath |
| Togs | Clothes |
| Toov | Tobacco/cigarettes |
| Traveller | Gypsy |
| Trolley man | Man who races horses and ponies in trotting matches |
| Trotting match | Horse-and-cart race |
| Vardo | Trailer/caravan/wagon |
| Wad | Money |
| Wedge | Money |
| Weigh on | Pay/repay |
| Wonga | Money |
| Wrongun | Grass/police informer |
| Yocks | Eyes |
| Yog | Fire |
| Yogga | Gun |

# INTRODUCTION

# I

**GYPSIES, PIKEYS, TRAVELLERS OR DIDICOIS,** call them what you will, were a familiar part of the social landscape where we were born and raised around Mitcham and Epsom in Surrey, England. In fact Epsom, romantically at least, could well be described as the spiritual home of the gypsy due to the long association between the Derby, Britain's most famous horse-race, and the annual gathering of gypsies from all over England and beyond. Part of Mitcham was known as Redskin Village because of the large numbers of Romanies who wintered in yards there, while travelling to Kent for hop-picking in the summer. Indeed, the 1888 census records at least one hundred gypsies living in 'bender' tents on Mitcham Common. Some of their descendants settled in the high-rise flats, which were built years later when the yards closed.

Inevitably, many gypsy families settled in Epsom too, and in the surrounding areas. Therefore, at school and on the council estates, we grew up with boys and girls whose families had, five, ten or fifty years before, been living in a caravan. The closer they were to coming off the gypsy encampments the more obvious their heritage was, but if it was a generation or two back, it was harder to tell. Two of our friends, who, unusually, shared the same christian and surnames, didn't discover until they were well into their twenties, and one of them began to trace the family tree, that they most likely had a great-grandfather in common, a gypsy who had settled in a hop-picking area of Kent.

At school, those two boys wouldn't have shouted about their gypsy blood even if they had known about it then, because the Romanies were a race apart – not in the same way as the jungle bunnies, the Pakis or the Chinks, as the other ethnic children were called at our schools in the more overtly racist 1960s and '70s, but nevertheless different. Unlike those other races, they were not easily identifiable by the colour of their skin or their family names and unlike the West Indians, Asians and Chinese, there were no concerted attempts by either side to integrate.

The fact was that gypsies, as an ethnic group, were ignored by so-called society altogether. There were no awareness programmes orchestrated from on high, no celebrations of their culture, no nothing. Here was a race steeped in history and tradition quite literally on our doorsteps, but zilch was taught to us about them in our schoolbooks or by our teachers. No one told us, for example, that many gypsy men, despite their aversion to rules and regulations of any kind, signed up and fought valiantly in the First and Second World Wars. Their skills as snipers and scouts were particularly appreciated. Some men, such as Jack Cunningham VC, went on to win medals for extreme bravery. Jesse Frankham, a member of a family frequently referred to in this book, was awarded the Croix de Guerre in the First World War after he went behind enemy lines on horseback, dressed as a German officer.

Gypsies had every reason for wanting to defeat Germany – during the Second World War, Hitler had a good go at wiping them out in mainland Europe, and apparently had detailed plans on how to round up the English gypsies when the Germans could finally be bothered to invade Britain.

The unspoken message communicated to us in our childhood was that these people were not wanted – were not to be embraced. It permeated downward; from politician to constituent, from teacher to pupil and from father to son. These prejudices appeared to be officially sanctioned, too. The week before the Derby, for example, the local Epsom papers would carry urgent warnings from the police, advising householders to be vigilant and to be wary of who they answered their doors to. The gypsies were in town. Even Cher, the singer whose looks owe more to the Red Indian or the Romany than the conventional American, lumped them in with tramps and thieves in a pop song from our youth.

Ordinarily, this could have been a licence for persecution or elimination by the majority. But the travellers we knew neither sought nor courted approval from non-gypsies. They were what they were, and proud of it. There was no desire to foist their beliefs and way of life on others but they didn't expect, and weren't having any of, others interfering with them. It was as if they didn't care about outsiders. The fact that their culture has survived and they still manage, just about, to live by their own rules, regulations and ethics in this bureaucratic, nanny state age is testament to their durability, tenacity and toughness.

---

Toughness. That, more than anything, was what we knew them for. They may have been a minority group, like the Asians were in our youth, but no gangs took up 'gypo-bashing', or shouted abuse across the street to them. The truth was that we were scared of the gypsies, both as a race and as individuals. They were usually bigger, stronger and better fighters than us and they lived outside the laws and world that was ours. Therefore, there was no way peer pressure could be applied on them to conform. There was no getting your older brother or dad on to them, or threatening them with the law. The chances were they would have moved on anyway. Scrapping was second nature for these boys. They practised on each other, with their brothers, fathers and friends. And many a nattily dressed youth hailed locally as a hard case experienced his first defeat at the hands of a young traveller with greased-back Elvis hair, dressed in plain grey trousers, white shirt and braces.

Never did we question where they came from. How they got here. Where they'd been and where they were going. Partly, this was due to the gypsies' own lack of a written history and a vagueness about themselves, but mainly it was because 'officially', they were not a legitimate part of history or society.

Linguistic experts have established that the Romany originated in India (although, confusingly, the word 'gypsy' derives from the word 'Egyptian') and then made their way across Asia and Europe, splintering and developing into various sub-groups along the way. They are thought to have turned up in Britain in the 14th or 15th centuries. Settled societies didn't exactly welcome them with open arms, and probably created the negative legends and myths that surround them to this day. One such legend claims that it was gypsies who forged the nails to crucify Jesus Christ, and have therefore been condemned to perpetual wandering ever since. This didn't help their standing with Christians, no doubt. Another, more positive, story is that gypsies are the descendants of Adam and a first woman created before Eve; they were therefore born without original sin, and unlike the rest of mankind, are not condemned to work. It is estimated there are about five million gypsies living in Europe today, with about 100,000 resident in the UK. Although 'estimated' has to be the right word. The electoral roll, directory enquiries and the Registrar of Births, Marriages and Deaths hardly burst with information on the travelling classes.

---

A first memory of a gypsy for me was during Derby week. I was too young to be trekking up Epsom Downs to witness the event. A lady knocked on our door selling heather, lucky heather, she said. I hung on to my mum's apron strings as she begrudgingly fished some small change from her purse. I was intrigued by the lady's tanned, leathery face, framed in a scarf, and the sparkle in her eyes. I sensed, though, that my mum was uncomfortable. 'Is it really lucky?' I asked, examining the clump of heather that Mum had unceremoniously dumped on the kitchen table when the lady had gone.

'No, what the gypsy lady means is that if I don't buy any, I'll have bad luck. So I'm not taking any chances.'

Later, I became quite familiar with them up on Epsom Downs, and got to know the handful that came to our school from the local council-run gypsy site. Walking into the Derby fair, a schoolboy's paradise, we'd run the gauntlet of gypsy caravans, to gain entry to the rides and the coconut shies.

A gypsy man would accost all with what seemed an irresistible offer. 'Come on, boys, let me guess your age for a shilling. If I'm more than a year out either side, I'll give you 1/6d back.' Adults loved it. So that they couldn't cheat and simply deny the gypsy man's guess if he was correct, they had to write down the age on a slip of paper, fold it and hand it to an assistant. The old gypsy man won seven times out of ten. I know, because I stood and watched to see how he did it and whether I could spot any trickery, but I never could. Looking back on it now, I suspect that the old gypsy man could be relied upon to guess the decade any punter was in, and the assistant probably had a way of signalling the number, after a sneaky look at the paper.

Most of the gypsies touting for business at the fair were women though. Old, faded posters leant up against fantastically shining caravans, announcing that the lady inside was a direct descendant of Gypsy Rose Lee. This fabled gypsy lady seemed to have a great deal of direct descendants advertising their mystic wares on Epsom Downs. They would read your palm, or tell your fortune from a crystal ball. Pinned on the windows were dog-eared photographs of Pat Phoenix (Elsie Tanner of *Coronation Street* fame), Terry Dene and other half-remembered '50s personalities, standing next to or outside the fortune-teller's caravan smiling nervously. They charged ten bob, which was beyond our purses, or would have severely dented our rides-and-chips money, so we never ventured inside.

---

A decade later, as a young man, I witnessed a bare-knuckle fight between two gypsies. This was the stuff of urban myth. We'd all heard about the bare-knuckle marathons held on Epsom Downs, attended by thousands, somehow without the knowledge of the authorities. My friend, working as a stable lad for one of the Epsom horse racing trainers, stumbled on a fight at dawn one morning. He saw a crowd some hundred strong in one of the dips on the Downs, invisible from the road. Leaving his string he trotted over to the scene and was shooed away, but not before seeing two men, stripped to the waist, bashing hell out of one another.

My own experience was after the Oaks meeting, around 1977. I was pleased with myself because my girlfriend and I had won a few quid on the winner, a horse called Dunfermline. We were hanging around with a few friends outside the Rubbing House pub as the last of the race-goers headed off to catch the bus, or to begin the downhill trek to Epsom town centre and the railway station. Policemen filed into their vans, helmets clasped under their arms, and the racecourse area began to empty almost as quickly as it had been filled hours earlier.

As we drained our lager from plastic pint glasses, we noticed a large crowd forming in the dip below the racecourse, where the old fair used to be held. Someone said a prize-fight was about to start. We finished our drinks and hurried over, as did almost everyone else in the area.

The two men were already in a bloody state by the time we pushed ourselves into a viewing position. They were both stripped to the waist, and were not wearing gloves. The sound of flesh and bone cracking down on flesh and bone made me wince, but what disturbed me more were the ages of the two opponents. One was a boy and one was a man. I didn't know who to feel sorry for. The boy was about my age, 19 or 20, and he was not particularly tall or big. The man, though, was around 40 years of age, and huge. A beer gut hung over his trousers which, I noticed, were held up with string, and the muscles in his huge arms rippled. His fists were like the proverbial sledgehammers. But the boy was fit and seemed versed in boxing technique – he flitted around the older man and flicked out punch after punch, avoiding his opponent's flailing fists. Technically the older man was being embarrassed; the boy was making a monkey out of him. It was obvious, though, that he had landed one or two telling blows on junior before we'd got there: the skin under the boy's eye was flapping and leaking blood. Every now and then a referee parted them, and a second jumped out of the crowd, soaked up the blood from the boy's wound with a sponge and then stepped back into the throng. 'What's it all about?' I enquired of a pretty gypsy girl standing next to us. 'It's family business,' she said aggressively.

Soon a police carrier came careering across the grass, scattering the bed of race-goers' rubbish in its wake, and the fight crowd began to run as one across the Downs in the direction of Headley. In the mêlée, a pony that was tied to a post outside a caravan panicked and attempted to bolt but appeared to break its own neck. We stopped and stared hopelessly as the pony jerked in agony on the floor. The owner came out of his trailer and delivered a mercy blow to his pony with a lump of wood and then looked over at us accusingly.

The crowd had disappeared over the horizon towards Langley Vale, where the fight was obviously going to be resumed. But we'd seen enough violence in just a few minutes to want to step back into our safer little world. As we sat upstairs on the green bus home, we stayed silent. The images of the dying pony and the determined young boy with the flapping face loomed in our minds. For all I know, that boy could have been the young Jimmy Stockin.

# II

That bare-knuckle fight I glimpsed on Epsom Downs was merely the latest in a centuries-old tradition. In fact, a famous match took place there following a race meeting in 1771 between two well-known pugilists of the time – Peter Corcoran and Bill Darts. For the record, Darts was accused of throwing the fight. However, bare-knuckle fighting as a spectator sport had been established in England at least a century before that contest. Samuel Pepys records, in his famous diary, spectating at a bout in Westminster, London, in 1660.

By the time of the Corcoran fight, the more localised and brutal (inasmuch as the contestants didn't have a big say in the matter) pastimes of cockfighting and the dog pit, widely popular in the Middle Ages, had been marginalised in favour of cricket and horse racing. These latter sports were patronised by rich and poor alike. Only bare-knuckle, or prize-fighting (as it was also called if prize-money was put up for the eventual victor), survived among the combative blood sports. The differences between cock or dog fighting and bare-knuckle were not as marked as one may imagine. Modern boxing, which evolved from prize-fighting, owes its ten-second countdown for a knockout to original cockfighting rules.

A fighter by the name of Jack Broughton is credited with developing bare-knuckle fighting from a tacky fairground attraction to a national sport patronised by royalty, with fighters whose fame was as close as the 18th century would allow to that of David Beckham or Robbie Williams. Broughton, besides being a mean fighter himself, set up an amphitheatre and began staging fights for himself and other contemporary players to draw in the paying crowds. Soon, he was making good money and he could number among his customers dukes and princes. One of the names who fought in Broughton's amphitheatre was Gypsy 'Prince' Boswell, which suggests that gypsy bare-knuckle fighters were very much part of the prize-fighting scene, even in those formative years.

Most importantly, perhaps, Broughton formalised the rules of the sport. These rules still hold today, even though the Marquis of Queensberry's intervention, a century later, would take boxing of the gloved variety off in a different direction. Broughton was also ahead of his time in encouraging his men to use mufflers, or light gloves, in training, to limit the damage they could do to one another. His rules were fairly straightforward and are taken for granted nowadays, but included such dictates as no man should be in the ring besides the two opponents and the seconds, and that no person is to hit his adversary when he is down on the floor. This gives some indication of what was acceptable before Broughton came along. In fact, early prize-fighting was a mixture of fist fighting and a vicious form of wrestling.

Initially, the ring really was a ring and not the square that we are familiar with today in modern boxing. A line was scratched in the middle of the ring, and the two opponents would have to approach this before the fight commenced. From this, the saying 'coming up to scratch' or 'not up to scratch' has been derived. Prize-fighting has enriched the British language in many instances, and this demonstrates how popular and widely accepted the sport was. The expression 'stake money' derives from the practice of attaching the purse for a fight to one of the stakes which would have had rope wound around and between them to form a ring for the early fighters. 'Whips' were men who wielded short whips to dissuade the crowd from encroaching on the fighting area. Afterwards, it was their task to contribute to a collection for the boxers. From this, the saying 'whip-round' entered the English language. 'Seconds' were literally used as the second boxers. If the first fight ended early, these men would be expected to provide a second fight.

Probably the most famous saying to emerge from bare-knuckle customs is 'throwing one's hat into the ring'. This occured when the travelling prizefighters would take on all comers for money, an early version of the fairground boxing booths which survived until around 30 years ago. To signify that they fancied their chances against the prizefighter, the local village men would throw their hats into the ring.

Things started to go wrong for Broughton in 1750, when he fought a nobody called Jack Slack. The Duke of Cumberland was said to have backed Broughton to the tune of £10,000 (over half a million pounds in today's money) at odds of 10–1 on. Broughton took a smack between the eyes, which nearly blinded him, and the fight was lost – as was the Duke's money. The Duke was understandably miffed and within weeks, Broughton's amphitheatre was closed down and prize-fighting was driven underground, back to the streets, meadows and fairgrounds.

Royalty may have temporarily spurned the sport, but the common people still loved it and big name fights would attract huge crowds, with all their attendant problems. The fights encouraged the working classes to abandon their honest toil, and rowdiness and brawling often accompanied the spectacle. At least, that's how the aspiring ruling classes saw it. Parliament wasted no time in outlawing prize-fighting. Meanwhile, horse racing prospered as the leading spectator sport, and soon prize-fighting attached itself, unofficially, to this more socially acceptable pastime. Big bouts took place at courses across the country, often before or after the day's racing – a tradition that has survived to this day. Sky Television hasn't latched on yet, but no doubt one day they will.

In the last quarter of the 18th century, a star emerged in the form of a flamboyant Jewish man called Daniel Mendoza. He established nationwide fame with his antics and impressive physique. His fights were reported in *The Times* and sporting journals of the time, and his charisma attracted back the patronage of the aristocracy. By the turn of the century, after a long and successful career, John Jackson defeated Mendoza, who was later reduced to touring the music halls giving exhibition bouts. The large amounts of money he had earned during his long career were drunk away and he died penniless in Petticoat Lane, East London, in 1836. His natural charm, wit and talent at playing to an audience resurfaced some three generations later. Mendoza's great-grandson was Peter Sellers.

During the first part of the 19th century, for no obvious reason, the sport became dominated by Bristol and West Country men: Jem Belcher, Henry Pearce, John Gully, Tom Cribb and Tom Spring among them. It could have been in the blood – Jem Belcher, for example, was the grandson of Jack Slack, the man who had temporarily blinded Jack Broughton years before. Jem Belcher is considered by many boxing experts to be one of the greatest pugilists ever, and his championship match against Joe Bourke attracted as much interest as any of Mendoza's great fights. When he retired, Belcher took over as landlord of the Jolly Brewers in Wardour Street, London, but died soon after at the age of 30. Life expectancy for fighters, then as now, was considerably less than the national average. Tom Cribb, one of the men to hasten Belcher's decline, was said to be the first champion to employ scientific training methods.

By now, crowds of 10,000 or more were not uncommon for the high-profile bouts, and the stars could accumulate real wealth if they were careful. The aforementioned John Gully was particularly adroit: retiring from the game before he became too injured, he turned to horse racing as a gambler and later as a racehorse owner. His turf career peaked in 1854 when he won the 2,000 Guineas with a horse called Hermit, and the Epsom Derby with Andover.

Although prize-fighting was probably at its most popular in the early 19th century, it was still illegal and promoters played a constant game of cat-and-mouse with the sheriffs and the police when they attempted to stage a contest. For one fight in 1819, a 20,000-strong crowd assembled on Wimbledon Common, only to be told the venue had been switched to Hounslow. At Hounslow, the site was moved yet again to nearby Colnbrook. Such movement of large, rowdy crowds on foot, horseback and in rickety carriages alarmed the authorities, who reacted by becoming more and more determined to stop what they saw as a disgusting and unsavoury pastime, enjoyed by the riffraff. Again, the sport entered a period of decline.

Fight followers were not easily deterred, however, and in an interesting parallel with the 20th-century football fan, they utilised the newly constructed Victorian railway network. Fight organisers (19th-century Frank Warrens, if you like) chartered special excursion trains and took the fighters and their spectators across the English countryside. At an appropriate juncture, possibly when 'entrance' money had been collected from all and sundry, the train would stop, its human contents spill out and the fight would be had in some green field on the edge of an unsuspecting village or hamlet.

Newspapers sensationally reported these invasions of rowdy Londoners, and described how they fought one another and drank sleepy rural villages dry. Eventually, the fledgling Metropolitan Police would patrol the main-line stations, such as London Bridge, on the fight days, and travel with the hordes on the trains in an attempt to keep order. This was something their descendants would be doing a century later with the football crowds as they followed their teams around the country on the notorious 'soccer specials'. Little did these modern-day policemen know that their ancestors were dealing with a very similar phenomenon in the first days of the Met. Eventually parliament stepped in, as it does, and banned rail excursions to prize-fights.

The middle and latter parts of the 19th century produced such fighting names as William 'The Tipton Slasher' Perry, Tom Sayers and Jem Mace, but even these legends could not arrest the decline of bare-knuckle fighting as a spectator sport. (Sayers had an enduring career, appearing in the ring 16 times between 1849 and 1860. Bearing in mind the ferocity of these contests – they sometimes lasted hours – this was a considerable achievement. Doctors have likened the trauma suffered by bare-knuckle fighters in a competitive fight to a fairly serious car crash. Sayers, therefore, had the equivalent of 16 head-on smashes in 11 years.) Crowds and interest dwindled, and many fighters, including the highly popular Jem Mace, sailed over to America where the sport was in its ascendancy and, more importantly, legal and lucrative. Australia took to it too, after it was introduced by English convicts who had been shipped out there in the 19th century.

Jem Mace was the last British-bred nationally famous bare-knuckle fighter. He was a Norfolk boy, who learnt his trade in the fairground boxing-booths, taking on the inebriated and the brave. When he travelled to America, he beat the native Tom Allen and should really have been crowned champion of the world, but because he was officially retired it didn't seem to count. Mace moved on to Australia, where he gave sparring exhibitions, and shocked onlookers by giving a startling account of himself in a competitive sparring match with the young championship contender, Dick Burge, when he was 64 years of age.

Mace also coached, and one of his student protégés was Bob Fitzsimmons, who went on to become a gloved heavyweight champion of the world, providing a telling link between today's technical gloved fighters and the bone-crunching bare-knuckle age of fighters with fearsome nicknames like The Tipton Slasher.

During his career, Mace was dubbed 'The Swaffham Gypsy'. Swaffham was the nearest town to his home village of Beeston in Norfolk, and is still home to a gypsy settlement to this day. Mace denied having any Romany blood in him at all, although he conceded that one of his brothers married a gypsy girl. However, by all accounts, he had the looks and the traits of a Romany, and it is generally felt that his denial of Romany blood had more to do with his concern over his career and a desire to be seen as racially acceptable than anything else.

In his recently rediscovered autobiography, Mace recounts his fight with the so-called King of the Gypsies of the time. His name was Farden Smith, and they fought on Norwich Hill. In another parallel with today's bouts, the fight was interrupted by the police as they tried to break up the huge crowds that had gathered, and the two fighters had to make themselves scarce to avoid arrest. They resumed the following day at Mousehold Heath, a gypsy encampment, and Mace describes his nervousness about the venue. It turned out that Farden Smith gave his best before they even started fighting, but the two turned to drinking and merry-making for the rest of the day. The boxer who denied being a gypsy refers to it as one of his most memorable and enjoyable days.

Mace's explanation of how he became a prize-fighter is worth recounting. As a boy, he developed skills at playing the fiddle and one day whilst playing outside a public house for pennies, a group of three men jeered at him. One snatched the instrument from his hand, and smashed it to smithereens beneath his feet. The young Mace proceeded to beat the man with his fists, and when he was done with him, he then despatched his two friends. The fight was witnessed by a rich man, who was so impressed he took the young boy under his wing and on to meet a London fight promoter. Now if that isn't a gypsy story, what is?

Prize-fighting prospered across the Atlantic at least, and in 1882 when a local bare-knuckle boxer called John L. Sullivan beat Tug Wilson, the recognised British champion, his claim to be the first world champion was not disputed. A follow-up fight in Chicago against Jack Burke attracted a paying crowd of 12,000. Meanwhile, on the same day, two British prize-fighters fought at Charlton in London for £10, in front of only 40 people.

Although the Marquis of Queensberry Rules had appeared some 20 years before, the prize-fighting establishment had resisted introducing them, regarding the rules as an unnecessary sanitisation of an exciting sport. However, when John L. Sullivan decided that he would only defend his title in a gloved fight and under Queensberry Rules, boxing as we know it was born. His celebrated fight against James J. Corbett in 1892 took place in a floodlit arena before a crowd of 10,000, and marked the beginning of a new era. Jack Johnson, Jack Dempsey, Gene Tunney, Rocky Marciano, Muhammed Ali and Mike Tyson would all follow.

As far as the history books are concerned, prize-fighting was dead. But, as is often the case, history only records what it wants. Bare-knuckle *has* survived. The AFP press report (see opposite page) although typically sensationalised, could have been written about a fight from Daniel Mendoza's day – yet they are referring to Dublin, Ireland, at the end of 1999.

Throughout the 20th century, fights have been held on racecourses,

## 'King of the gypsies' bare-knuckle fights foiled

## AFP, 17 December 1999

In Dublin, a major operation by Irish police prevented a series of bare-knuckle fights due to have been held today to decide who was to be declared King of the Gypsies, a police spokesman said. More than 200 police were drafted into the North Midlands region and roadblocks were set up after police received information that 12 travellers were to do battle for the title in County Longford.

In recent court cases, there has been evidence that video recordings of these bruising fights are a lucrative business for members of Irish traveller clans. One member of the McDonagh clan was described as the 'Rupert Murdoch' of pay-per-view bare-knuckle fights. People are charged $US20 to watch them on giant video screens in New York.

Originally, the title of the top fighter was King of the Tinkers, but this has now been changed to the politically correct King of the Travellers. The title brings a certain prestige in the community, and higher prize-money for the holder.

Garda [police] Superintendent Tom Murphy said he had received information that a minority of travellers 'hell-bent on reckless violence' were planning to use bare-knuckle matches as an excuse for severe violence. 'The information was very specific. There was to have been a contest between 12 males, and the winner was to be declared the King of the Travellers. After that contest was over, the losing side were prepared to take very violent action,' he told Irish radio news. His men, who were backed up by units with police dogs and had helicopter support, seized a sawn-off shotgun, machetes, hatchets, knives and farm implements.

The police are increasingly concerned about the mounting violence in bitter feuds between clans, which mainly erupts at weddings and funerals.

on farmland and on gypsy sites. They are routinely beamed by satellite to America for hungry audiences. Results, accounts of fights and legends about the warriors are passed from person to person in pubs, at fairs and anywhere the working and travelling classes gather. Legends have sprung up around good men, bad men and brave men – men whose fame has spread across the country, yet their names appear in no record books, nor feature in any films. Their fame is of a special kind bestowed by the people who have seen them in action. Not for them the transient and empty celebrity of the jumped-up Hollywood star or the overpaid soccer player. Their impression on their public has been made through the sound of cracking jaws, the sight of spurting blood and raw courage, as they have bravely fought to win, for themselves and their supporters. People who see it don't forget it. These fighters command a well-earned and genuine respect among their own. Jimmy Stockin is one of those people. This is his story.

**Martin King**
**and Martin Knight**
**August 2000**

# 1.

# WHEN THE GOING GETS TOUGH

**I WASN'T THAT PISSED,** but I'd had a few pints this night and I was mellow, driving home from a friendly pub with a bit of music drifting out from the cassette player. As I turned the motor into the road leading to the site where I was pulled up, lights started coming on in trailers all over the place. Something was going on. As I pulled into the site, I could see figures moving around in the darkness. Turning the cassette off and winding the window down, I heard women screaming and hollering. It's going off, I thought, maybe the gavvers are here again making themselves busy.

Stopping outside Mum's place, I see my mother and sisters arguing with another family from a nearby trailer. I wind the window up and get one leg out the car. 'What the fuck is going on?' A blow comes down on the very top of my head, feeling like it has pushed my nut down into my body like a Jack-in-the-box. Before I can think about it, I've taken a couple more thumps to my temple and feel warm blood trickling down my cheek.

Managing to free my leg from inside the car, I stand up and get away from the open door, but this just makes me a better target. Accurate and telling blows are coming in fast, all to my face. I get one back in and feel the bones of my knuckles connecting with my attacker's flesh before another punch connects with my jaw and I'm going down. Don't think I'm sparked, because I remember it. Sliding down the wing of my old Corsair. My sheero cracking against the metal tyre rim. The head's pumping blood, but at least I've got a few seconds to get myself together.

Scrambling to my feet and trading punches, I see now who it is laying into me. 'Creamy, you cunt. What's up?' No reply, just a flurry of blows.

Creamy is a neighbour. I know him well – we've never had a problem before. He's only young, three or four years my junior. Nineteen probably, but already he is a well-known face in travelling circles as an up-and-coming young fighter.

The sound of sirens pierces the night air, followed in seconds by blue flashing lights swirling down the lane. The crowd that has gathered scurries off to the safety of their own trailers and the lights go off everywhere, almost as if there is a central switch. Four cars screech in. The garlos only ever come onto the site mob-handed. They're leaping out the cars and shining their torches between the caravans, but all they can see is a completely peaceful and empty gypsy encampment. And they ain't about to start knocking anyone up either, to find out what's been going on. It's rude to wake up people when they are asleep in bed. They know that.

Back in Mum's trailer, she and the girls give my cracked head some attention with plasters and creams, and fill me in on what has happened. There's been an argument between the female sides of our families, and it has got out of hand. Tonight, it has been stepped up a gear. My nut is fucking pounding, but not half as much as my heart, which wants revenge. Nothing is going to happen now, though. Not with the Old Bill outside, half-thinking that this might be the day when finally all the gypsies march into Epsom town centre with their flaming torches and burn the town to the ground.

The following morning my head is still throbbing, and looking in the mirror, I see a panda staring back. Two black eyes, a swollen mouth, cuts on my forehead and a gash on the back of my head where I've headbutted the car. Creamy is off the site for a few days after our run-in and the girls have all calmed down. Life settles down to an uneasy quiet, but I know this thing isn't finished, and so does Creamy.

A few days later, he appears at my trailer door, with Kenny Symes and Beetle Jim by his side. These two are well-known and respected bare-knuckle fighters, and I am surprised, and a bit alarmed, to see them. 'Fight me now,' demands Creamy, his temper flaring. I'm the one who should have the hump – after all, I'm the one who is black and blue! 'Let's see who is the best man, Jimmy,' challenges Creamy again.

I won't back down from no man, but I ain't no dimelow. If I fight Creamy now, I know I won't last long. These cuts on my face would open up like a flasher's zip. Also, deep down, I knew I had to get ready for this boy. He was a top fighter. Not only was he big and strong, he was ruthless and skilful. A dangerous combination.

'Give me one month. Let's get it on one month from today. That way you can get ready, and I can heal up some.'

Creamy probably didn't need to get ready. By the look of his fierce and flashing eyes, he was more than ready now. Kenny Symes looked at me. He could see my face was still in a state, and he knew what I was saying was fair – Kenny is a fair man. The fight was arranged for 30 days' time on a travellers' site – the Lonesome site, on the Mitcham/Streatham border. We all stood and nodded firmly to one each other, and then the three of them turned, walked away and got into their car.

Word went around like wildfire that we were fighting. There are bare-knuckle fights every week on sites up and down the country, borne from arguments, drink and bravado, and then there are the classics. Ordinary fights are had there and then. Only people in the immediate vicinity get to watch and after a few minutes, some blood and a few broken teeth, hands are shaken and all is forgotten. Classic fights are arranged, and are between good, highly rated fighters who will attract crowds and money. Me and Creamy's fight was going to be a classic. We were both well known among the travelling and fighting circles.

I knew that for my own self-respect and my family's honour, I had to get myself in top condition and give this my best shot. Immediately, I knocked the drink and the fags on the head and got myself running. Out of the site, through Epsom town centre and then uphill on the Ashley Road to Epsom Downs and back again. I felt that this alone would not be enough, so I got myself up the famous Thomas à Becket pub/gym on the Old Kent Road, and paid a trainer £60 to get me in condition. He was a great old geezer and had me sparring hundreds of rounds, with men of all weights and sizes. Then he'd get me pounding on the old, worn and torn punch bag that swung from the ceiling, and then back in the ring. As the 30 days passed, I felt better and better. My body felt good and so did my mind. I began to feel confident – but there was something missing.

Someone, actually. My younger brother Wally. He had been with me through thick and thin. He would die for me, as I would for him. But Wally was in prison on remand, and wouldn't be able to make the fight. If he'd been around I'd be as sharp as a pin, because Wally and me would have sparred every minute of the day. We sparred like other brothers might have a chat. He was a great fighter in his own right, smaller than me but fearless, fast and forever working on his boxing skills.

It broke me up going to visit Wally in Pentonville prison and seeing him upset over not being able to be with me when I faced my biggest test yet. He knew how much I needed him.

Wally wasn't sure why Creamy had visited me with the two fighting men, and advised me to go and see Mark Ripley and ask him to ensure that fair play was upheld. Mark was a fighting man who commanded respect among the gypsy community and gorgers alike. He reassured me that he would see fair play and would not allow any liberties to be taken before, during or after the fight. He also volunteered to be one of the referees, which pleased me. With a man like Mark involved, I felt settled and ready to spend my last few hours preparing for the fight. Although Mark and me knew of each other, it wasn't until after the fight with Creamy that we became good friends. A better friend you could not ask for. See – Wally did manage to help me after all.

The evening before the fight, I set out for my last run. I was feeling good and ready and I ran effortlessly all over, eating up the miles. I stopped in the garden of the Spring pub in Ewell Village and drank a couple of bottles of Pils lager. As I looked over at a couple of swans gently gliding across the pond, I reflected that this time tomorrow it would all be over. Chances were that both me and Creamy would be bashed up, but one of us would be the victor. I didn't bother running the mile back. I strolled home, climbed into bed and slept like a log.

When Les Stevens sounded his horn as he pulled up outside the trailer the following morning, I was already up, showered and dressed. Les was a good friend and a former professional boxer who had won the Southern Area heavyweight title some time before. He had also fought the Liverpudlian champion, John Conteh, in a professional fight, losing only on points. With him was his dad, Blue and my cousin Johnny Brazil, who gave me a reassuring grin as I climbed into the motor. Apparently, another fight had been arranged between Johnny and Creamy's brother, who went by the name of Champ. If Wally'd been out it would have been him, but Johnny was my cousin, and the next best thing. I suppose they were expecting a lot of spectators, and wanted to make it a good bill.

Not a lot was said on the car journey over to Streatham. Les and Johnny knew I didn't really want to talk – they had been there before. Nevertheless, Les asked if I had a bet on myself. I hadn't, but I would have. I had offered Creamy a straight £300, but he declined because he was skint. Was that an omen? Could it mean he wasn't sure? I soon dismissed the thought from my mind. Creamy may have still been in his teens, but he was a bull of a man, standing around 6ft 3ins with an impressive physique. Us gypsies mature early. We go from nappies straight into long trousers and braces. By the time you're 14 you're a man, and you have to live as a man. Like myself, Creamy came from a long line of fighters and he was determined to dispose of me. No prize-money or stakes were required to drive this fight. It was about family pride. Nothing more, nothing less.

No more was said. Line upon line of red-brick council houses flashed across my vision as we motored through Rose Hill, reputedly one of the biggest council estates in England, and headed down towards Mitcham. I felt pretty calm as we veered into the camp and parked the motor, but my stomach tightened when I saw the number of people crammed into the place. I'd never fought in front of so many. I wasn't scared – more shy. Someone shouted, 'He's here!'

Creamy appeared in the doorway of Kenny Symes's trailer and nodded over at me. There was a faint grin on his face. The look said, 'So you've turned up, then?' but I could be wrong. Did he think I was going to bottle it?

Creamy stepped down from the trailer, stripped to the waist and walked to the middle of the yard. He looked what he was – a fit heavyweight boxer. I took my shirt off and handed it to someone standing behind me, then loosened the elastic around the waist of my tracksuit bottoms. Then I stood and waited for the 300-odd people to gather around us and form the circle of bodies that would be our fluid ring. The space created would be three or four times the size of a normal boxing ring, and because its boundaries were human, had the novelty of being able to move around with the fighters. There was no canvas floor: hit the deck here and there was no soft landing, just damp and oil-stained concrete.

I clapped my hands together to signal I was ready, and looked out at the sea of faces studying Creamy, then me, then Creamy. Cauliflower ears, broken noses and facial scars were the order of the day. Travellers, gorgers, hard men, monied men – they were all here. All tense and waiting. Many would have money riding. Others were supporting their man. Some just liked seeing blood.

Kenny Symes and Mark Ripley came into the centre and asked for hush. The crowd fell obediently silent. There was no going back now – this was it. Win or lose, this fight was going down in gypsy folklore. Kenny beckoned us together, and we stared into one another's souls for just a second.

---

We square up in the orthodox boxing stance, and we're off. Crunch. I can't believe this is happening as Creamy's first punch – a big right-hander – puts me straight on my arse. How embarrassing. It's almost enough to shame me into giving best here and now. But I scramble almost immediately to my feet. I'm mumbling, 'I'm all right, I'm all right.' I want people to know that it was just a lapse of concentration, not a fundamental problem. But I feel a wanker for going down like that straightaway.

My head clears a bit as Creamy gets some more pokes in and I start finding my ground, although I'm not making much of an impression. He's running the show for the first ten minutes. Creamy is fighting behind a sharp, solid jab and a high left hand covering his face. The jab keeps flicking out as he dances around me and I can feel my face reddening up, beginning to swell. But I'm on him and moving in close, slowly feeling my way into the fight. My spirits are lifted when a left-right left-right combination gets through Creamy's guard. I follow it through with a crunching left hook, and his expression changes. I can see I've hurt him. 'Have some of that, you Welsh cunt!' I spit at him.

'Get fucked, Stockin – you're fuck all!' retorts Creamy.

The fight continues at a measured pace. Neither of us is going to risk getting exhausted too early. We're hitting each other but we're not taking chances, and since Creamy's first punch, he hasn't opened up on me nor I on him.

Smack. Smack. Two hard shots from me land perfectly on his ribs, and I know they've done some damage. I never planned it beforehand, but once I'd been fighting Creamy a few minutes, I knew I had to get to work on his body. Getting to his head was uphill work and would kill me within a quarter of an hour. Keep working the body, and hopefully his head might come down as he searches for breath. Creamy's strategy was obviously the opposite – work my head. Work it until I go down and stay down.

Jab after jab from Creamy hits home and each one stings. If they had a camera on me you'd see the bruises coming up, like when they speed up the film on those wildlife television documentaries, and you see a flower blooming.

As I gulp for air, he catches me with a whipping right hand which rocks me backwards. Blood trickles into my eye. Instinctively brushing it away with the back of my left hand, I glance at it to make sure before wiping it off on my tracksuit bottoms. It is the fight's first blood, and the sight of it gives Creamy a lift. He cranks up the pace, gives more good hits to my face. Claret is now trickling down the bridge of my nose. I shake my face, like a dog emerging from a river, to try and get the blood off, and keep coming forward, trying to make out the blood is not a problem.

I sink two heavy shots into his ribs. One of them punches felt different: I think I may have cracked a rib, but Creamy's not showing the pain, although I am backing him up for the first time – looking for an opening. Getting put on the back foot in a bare-knuckle fight is a bad thing. As there is no ring and the crowd moves with you, a fighter can end up covering miles. Counter-punchers don't often make good bare-knuckle men, but Creamy is no counter-puncher. He's not on the back foot for long. His sheer determination and strength pulls him back.

It is like a chess match. I wish it *was* a fucking chess match. Right now, I envy the professional boxers, with their rules and regulations and watchful doctors on hand. Oh for a breather every few minutes, when the bell rings. Please give me my second in the corner, refreshing me, cascading cold water over my head and down my dry throat. Please give me my man, gently wiping the blood away, encouraging me and comforting me. Oh for a stool where I can park my arse for a minute or two and take the weight off these tired legs, whilst my man pampers me with a fluffy, warm towel. He'd be there telling me where I'm going wrong or right, and he'd save my pride if he saw I was done. Stop me being brain-damaged, or even killed, by throwing the towel in. But no way. This is boxing stripped down to the bare bones. To the bare knuckles.

Creamy sends a crashing right to my chin, but I see it at the last millisecond and turn. His sledgehammer fist connects with my ear instead. The pain is worse than all the blows in the rest of the fight put together. The ear feels like it's hanging off, and the agony rush sends alerts all over my body. I'm literally covered in blood now, caked up in the stuff. I daren't look down, but it's all over the concrete. My chest is streaked red and my fists are stained with claret as I constantly try to clear my eyes and wipe my face. Keep going, Jim. Wish Wally was here.

I'm ducking under Creamy's blows and banging into his stomach. But for every good body shot I get in, I'm presenting him with three or four clear punches to my head. I can't see a happy ending somehow. How long have we been fighting? It feels like an age. Don't know how long either of us can go on. We've tested each other to the extreme: my eyes are closing up and Creamy looks like he's under pressure. The thought of quitting goes through my mind, and I vainly hope Mark or Kenny steps in and calls it a draw. Honours, even. But it don't work like that.

Then the sky starts to grey up and it begins to spit, building into a drizzle and then a steady rain. It washes me down. Dislodges the clumps of blood. Soothes my stinging ear. The rain is a real tonic for me, and I feel renewed. Must watch my footing though, as the floor gets wet and slippery.

For me, the rain is the turning point. We're both losing our ground as we step backward to avoid each other's blows. The crowd moves with us. We've swept about so much that even they must be getting tired. I can't believe how this bloke can keep throwing them out, though. His punches have lost none of their snap. He's either trained hard, or he's a fitter fucker than I ever imagined. The blood is in my eyes and I can barely see.

One, two, three, four, five. Creamy's punches hit home, jerking my head one way, then the other. How much more can I take? One, two, three – there is no four or five this time. I crouch low as his fourth sails across the air where my head was, come up and screw a body shot right into his guts. My fist sinks deep into his solar plexus, and hits home so hard that shock waves reverberate all the way up my arm to the shoulder. Creamy staggers back a little and lets out a loud groan, like a tyre puncturing. Air and pain escape his body as one. Before I can move in and make the most from this unexpected turn in my favour, he drops his arms.

'That's it. I've had enough.'

If only he'd uttered those words some 45 minutes earlier.

---

The crowd was silent at first, then someone clapped and it spread like a ripple. They all joined in, cheering and clapping the two of us. Two gypsy warriors who had just fought like lions. Three-quarters of an hour we'd been fighting without a breather. Me and Creamy almost fell into an embrace after we shook hands. Mark, Les, Old Blue and Johnny could hardly contain their excitement as they congratulated me. Fellas I'd never met before stepped up and pressed their hands into my swollen and bruised ones, others ruffled my hair, and most of the crowd came up and patted my back before moving off to their trucks and cars.

Slipping my shirt on, I swigged from a bottle of water and savoured the sensation of the water soothing my battered gums and the bloody inside of my mouth. Following the cars off the site, someone decided we needed to have a celebratory drink in the Albion pub in Mitcham. I didn't really feel up to it, but was swept along on the adrenaline of winning.

Fifty or so men were already packing the public bar when we arrived. Light and bitters, lagers, brown and milds and Guinnesses were being passed over people's heads. The fight seemed to have given this lot some thirst.

'What you having, son?'

'Some fight there, boy.'

'You're up with the best of them now.'

All over the bar, the talk was about the fight. Everyone agreed it was a classic and that it would be talked about for years to come. Men re-enacted moves over their beer, telling each other where me or Creamy had gone wrong or right, how they would have played it.

'You should get to hospital, bruv, Creamy's gone up to be checked over already,' said an old gypsy man. Now the adrenaline buzz was subsiding, I had started to feel groggy. My head was a mass of bumps, I had two black and cut-up eyes, my nose was still bleeding and my lips were fat and bloody. Worst of all, though, my ear was throbbing like it had been amputated minutes before with a blunt machete. I decided to go home and let the family know I was okay.

My sisters were waiting outside my caravan, with my mum standing smiling behind them. As I got out the car they rushed up and hugged me. 'Well done, Jim,' Mum says gently as she strokes my sore head.

'How do you know I won?' I asked, because I couldn't have looked too clever.

'Mark Ripley's wife rang and told us.'

I sat on the steps of my trailer and tried to relax. A constant flow of well-wishers came along, the last one, in the early evening, being Creamy himself.

'Some fight, eh, Jim?'

'Some fight, Creamy.'

He told me he had a fractured wrist and a broken rib, but those injuries didn't stop him driving the two of us back down the Albion for a quiet drink together. We talked about the fight, wondered how much money had changed hands in wagers and told each other genuinely of the great respect we now had for one another.

The following day, I was in agony and I heard Creamy was the same way. He was laid up for some days as his body mended itself, and myself, I didn't work for two whole weeks. And it wasn't like I could afford not to work – that's how battered, bruised and drained I was.

---

Creamy and I remained firm friends. The bad blood had been spilt and washed away. He is a decent man, and a decent fighter. The thought of a rematch, had it had been suggested, would not have been on the top of my list of priorities. He turned professional later and had three fights. As far as I know, he was unbeaten. The night of the fight, though, after my quiet hour or two with the man I'd been up against earlier, I fell into my bed, tingling, aching and throbbing. But I couldn't wait to get up in the morning, drive up to Pentonville prison, and tell Wally all about it. How I hadn't let Dad down. I thought about Dad, wished he could have seen it, and fell off to sleep remembering how it all began.

# 2.

# TRAVELLING CHILD

**JUNE 1958. HARD RIDDEN** had won the Derby on Epsom Downs, with Charlie Smirke up. As a kid, I knew all the jockeys' names almost like family, because the men talked about them so often. The ones who were riding then, like Lester Piggott, Willie Carson and Joe Mercer, and the others that the older men remembered, like Smirke, Bill Rickaby, Scobie Breasley and Steve Donoghue. They often told us about a jockey called Fred Archer from over a hundred years before, who they said was the best ever man to ride a racehorse. But he shot himself dead, and now his ghost rides over Newmarket Heath.

Dad and a heavily pregnant Mum would have been there when Hard Ridden passed that famous winning post, him smiling and enjoying the sun, with the breeze in his hair and his white shirt-sleeves rolled up over the elbow. He'd have had a bet, no doubt, and would have drawn his winnings or forgotten his losses, before adjourning to the beer tent on the hill and sitting down with friends and family on upturned beer crates, telling stories, drinking and laughing. Some of my older cousins would have wandered over to the famous Derby fair, where the local Teddy Boys and young gypsies would be eyeing each other up cautiously, and the showmen cranked up the latest Everly Brothers or Elvis disc to attract the teenagers to their chairoplanes or dodgem cars.

Just a few weeks later, I came into the world and joined them all. My actual birthplace was Rose Hill Hospital, a sprawling expanse of white concrete, which was built to take the casualties from the Rose pub on a boozy Saturday night. I was Mum and Dad's third child, following my sisters, Betsy and Louie. Dad must have been over the moon. At last, the son he had dreamed of had arrived; a boy who could follow the family tradition of fighting.

It was all mapped out for me. Dad had been a fighter, as had his father. Various cousins and uncles had also been accomplished boxers and fighters. Some had fought professionally. Bare-knuckle was in the blood, though.

Muggy Stockins, as he was known, would have celebrated my arrival in the nearest pub. I know he had a few too many that night, because he pinched a pram for me, from a local scrap metal man on the way home. Mum was as pleased as punch with it, wheeling her little Jimmy around the site where we were staying.

Home, at this time, was a piece of land known locally as the Dust. It was smack bang in the middle of a large council estate in Mitcham, and there were only about 20 trailers pulled on there. The locals and the travellers, by all accounts, got on well. The estate, with us lot in the middle, had a fearsome, lawless reputation. The gavvers patrolled in pairs, debt collectors and rent men decided not to bother and ticked the 'Not at Home' box on their clipboards before moving on to their next call, and Jehovah's Witnesses converted back to whatever they were before, after visiting the estate.

The estate's nickname, Redskin Village, was said to have come from outsiders who likened it to a Wild West town, and said that if you ventured on to it, you'd likely be scalped. Others told a tale about Canadian soldiers setting up camp on the Dust during the last war and erecting teepees to live in.

The local pub was called the Bath Tavern, but everyone knew it as the Blood Tub or the Blood Bath Tavern. Fights were guaranteed around closing time, and only one type of woman dared venture inside.

All the houses around the Dust were being pulled down and blocks of flats were shoved up in their place. It didn't bear thinking about for those poor sods that had to live in them. It was bad enough all being crushed together side by side in kennas, but having families on top of you and families on top of them as well – no thanks. And as for us, in the centre, we'd all be overlooked like some flea circus. The pub was pulled down and replaced with a drab, single-storey, so-called modern thing and a row of identical grey shops. The green fields of Essex beckoned. We were on the move.

---

Dad found a disused airfield in Hornchurch which only had a few caravans on it, but word soon got round and within a couple of months it became a big site, with over 200 trailers. The gypsy grapevine was an important way of communicating. It was how we kept tabs on where each other was. Someone on a new site would tell us that they had seen our cousins on a site down near Worthing, for instance, and we'd think, right, we'll mosey on down there in a few days. It was incredibly efficient, really, considering there were no mobile phones, that at any given time everyone knew where everyone else was. English, Scottish and Welsh travellers lived happily side by side at the Hornchurch site – I can even remember a family of German gypsies living there for a while.

Brother Wally came along when we were there, and I was overjoyed to have another boy to play with. We wandered around freely, playing with our sisters, cousins and kids from other families, exploring the local countryside and learning about nature. In the evenings, we'd sit around a big, glowing fire and listen as the adults told says. We'd poke potatoes we'd collected during the day into the fire and eat them, burnt up and all.

The says were stories that made the hairs on the back of your neck stand on end. Stories which made you want to cry, and stories which would have us rocking with laughter. Many says, passed down the generations, were about how gypsies had won through against the odds or had outwitted a gorger man. The stories that Wally and me liked best, though, were about the great fights, classic fights the men had seen or even been in. The men would say the fighters' names with pride, and whistle admiringly through their lips as they pondered the skills or strength of this man and that man, men like Poshy Frank and our very own uncles Dido and Rymer.

It all seemed so romantic. We knew the stories behind the fights, each little detail, and we got to hear about the new duels when they happened. From tiny boys, we couldn't help but realise that bare-knuckle fighting was very important to the grown-ups and that the men who seemed to command the most respect and admiration among them were the best fighters.

One of the classic fights the men would speak of was between Tom Brazil and Jimmy Frankham. Tom was related to Dad, as was Jimmy, who was father of the Frankham boys, including Johnny, who would one day become a British boxing champion. In drink, the two of them came to fighting and Tom woke up in the morning pretty badly beaten and cut up. He was convinced that Jimmy could not have done that with his fists alone, and challenged him about it. Jimmy Frankham maintained he had only used his fists, and that it had been a fair straightener. Nevertheless, Tom was not satisfied, and suspected that knuckle-dusters, or something worse, had been used on him. A fight was arranged for when Tom's wounds had healed.

Rymer Smith, a much-respected man, and grandfather to my cousin and close friend Joe Smith, was asked to see fair play. Rymer had been a fighting man who had turned professional, and if the war had not come along, many thought he may well have made a champion. It was a bit awkward for Rymer, for Tom was his brother-in-law and Jimmy was his best pal. Jimmy and Rymer had nothing but admiration for each other. Both men have told me, in later years, that the other was the best man ever to take his shirt off.

By all accounts, when it got to Tom and Jimmy taking their shirts off, the two men had wonderful physiques and were both at the peak of their powers. The fight lasted half an hour, which in prize-fighting terms is not the longest, but all who saw it, and there were many hundreds watching, said that it was one of the all-time classics.

Poor Rymer couldn't bear to see his two friends damaging each other so, and eventually ended the fight. Neither man was declared the winner, although it has been handed down that Jimmy Frankham shaded it. Just. Tom was happy with that. He knew this time, without any doubt, that Jimmy had beaten him fair and square. They went back to Tom's old wagon, where his wife had been preparing a kettle iron steak, which was bent over the old fire cooking away. Tom's wife had to feed the family and said she'd have to make Jimmy a sandwich since there wasn't enough food in the pot, but Tom would have none of it, and scraped half his dinner on to Jimmy's plate.

The Frankhams had a big fighting history, long before Johnny Frankham made the chests of all gypsies swell with pride when he became British light-heavyweight champion in the 1970s. In the early part of the last century, Jo Frankham famously beat Bombadier Billie Wells to win the British Empire boxing title. Wells was famous for being the muscle man who banged the big gong at the start of all those old British Top Rank films.

Bill Jones is also remembered for being a good fighting man. He was in a pub in Aldershot one day, with my Uncle Wally and another man called John Kent. All three of them were capable street fighters, but Bill Jones was a bit special. There had been some argument over a ring involving Goer West, who also had a tough reputation among travellers. Goer arrived in the pub, announced he was scared of no man and, of all the people to pick on, he decided to take Bill Jones outside. Bill, the story goes, smashed him to bits. Bill Jones is about 65 now and is confined to a wheelchair following a stroke, but stories about him and all the other gypsy fighters get passed down from generation to generation.

It wasn't all stories about fights, by any means, that enchanted us so. Many centred on my older cousin Neville Smith, who was a charming man, genuinely loved by gypsies and gorgers alike. He didn't have a violent bone in his body, but he still had the competitive Romany instinct. He could sing beautiful. There was no stopping him when he started and no one uttered a word when he was in song. Once he challenged Joe Brown to a singing duel at a club. At the time, the pop singer was riding high in the charts with 'A Picture of You'. Joe Brown and his Bruvvers thought better of getting into a contest with Neville and his brothers! Tragically, Neville died aged only 35, in 1975, from a heart attack.

I loved the life. For us kids, we had not a care in the world. We had the fresh air, the fields and the rivers, but most of all we had each other. We were living a child's dream. It was strange, I suppose, to go to sleep in the Essex countryside where the people outside the camp spoke with a country twang, and then wake up in the morning where the locals talked to us in that weird Brummie accent, but that's what travelling was all about. And even when we stayed put on a site for a long while, it was still like one never-ending holiday. At the time, gorgers saved up all year to have a week on a caravan site – to live like we did. I can't imagine any of us putting our pennies away to have a week in a house! But to my horror, that's what Dad told us one day – we were moving into a house over Feltham way.

The thought of it upset me, and I couldn't understand why Dad was making us move into a house. Kennas were not for us, but there was a lot of pressure at the time to stop gypsies travelling and promises of a better life. Maybe Dad thought it was best for us kids.

Worse was to come. The next thing I knew, Mum and Dad sent me to school. What did I want to go to school for? School was for gorgers. Why should I learn to read and write? No other person I mixed with could. All school could do for me was ruin my day, but what Dad said went – you didn't argue.

Don't ask me the name of the school. All I remember is that it wasn't far from where we lived. I hated it. Sit still. Sit up straight. Single file. Fold your arms. It was like being in a fucking cage, all silly rules and saying prayers. When Wally started, he was put in the infants' school next door, while I was in the juniors. All that separated our respective playgrounds was a white line painted on the tarmac. Poor Wally. I could see him standing alone crying at playtime on his first day and I walked over and put my arm around his shoulder.

'It's all right, bruv. It gets better. You wait and see. I was like this on my first day too.' Wally stopped crying, looked up at me and smiled.

A teacher blew a whistle and we all scampered off into a queue to file back into the school. As I walked in, a teacher, Miss something-or-other, pulled me by the arm out of the line. 'Jimmy, you crossed the white line, you know that's against the rules.'

I told her about Wally – how he was only a baby and was upset. She wagged her finger at me and rattled on about rules being rules.

I honestly couldn't understand what was wrong with what I did, why she was getting so cross. I gave her some lip, something I would never have dared do to my Dad, Mum, uncles or aunties. We were brought up to respect our elders. Some we knew to have special respect for. If Dad said 'He's a good man' about someone, and then looked at me for a few seconds, I knew Dad wanted me always to respect and honour that person. If I was misbehaving, all Dad had to do was look over and I stopped dead in my tracks. He was firm but fair – same as Mum.

School, for me, didn't last much longer. Wally and me were the only gypsies there, and some people seemed to want to remind us of this all the time. I couldn't understand why them calling 'Gypsy' or 'Gypo' across the playground was meant to annoy me. After all, that's what I was. If I had shouted back 'South West Londoner' to them, I doubt it would have hurt. Gorger kids seemed to think we didn't like being travellers for some reason. Nothing could have been further from the truth.

All the same, I had plenty of gorger friends and, on the whole, we got on fine. Mum and Dad didn't like us going round their houses, though. In fact, it was forbidden. I suppose they worried about perverts and the like; at least on the sites you knew everyone inside out and anyone the least bit suspect would be banished from a site like that. Our parents had no fears for us there.

My school days ended when I got into a scrap with another boy, I can't remember how. The teacher pulled us apart and sent us to the headmaster. I remember waiting outside his office, not being worried at all. I was soon horrified when I got inside. The headmaster mumbled on for a minute, then unlocked a cupboard and pulled out a long, thin piece of wood with nobbles all the way up it. He swished it in the air a couple of times and told us to hold out our hands. Like an idiot I did. I should have walked out there and then, but he brought the thing down with all his might and I copped the mad look in his eyes. Apparently, he had been the governor of the nearby Feltham young offenders' prison and was finishing off his days here. I felt the tears prick the back of my eyes, but was fucked if I was going to let him see. What was a grown man doing striking seven-year-old kids with a big stick? I knew school was bad, but I wasn't expecting this.

'My dad's gonna muller you,' was all I could say as I turned around and let myself out of his office. It all happened so quickly. Even though I was only seven, if I had known he was going to do that I'd have walked out or tried to dodge him. Dad was furious when I told him. I had never seen him so angry. His hands trembled, I remember that. 'Jim, you ain't going back to school, son.' It was music to my ears. Shame that Dad wouldn't let me go down there with him in the morning, when he tried to drag the head across his desk but was restrained by the other teachers.

The house wasn't doing us any good at all. Dad's health was suffering from being cooped up, and none of us could get used to having this strange thing called an 'upstairs' or going into a little cupboard to have a shit. On the road, us men and boys would use a field or, if we were on site, a ditch well behind the settlement. We'd put up little tents for the women to use. In houses, neighbours didn't take too kindly to us cooking our food over an open fire in the back garden each night either, and the horses upset the local dog and cat population. Finally, Dad said 'That's enough.' He bought a new trailer and we were off travelling again.

I was pleased that I had survived a couple of years of schooling without learning a thing, knowing that I would never set foot inside one again. There is one good side effect of us not reading and writing – when did you ever see a gypsy wearing glasses? We don't need them.

We don't strain our eyes reading books and filling out forms, that's why. Mind you, another theory is that standing in front of the bonfire is another reason not many gypsies need spectacles. Dad believed that the smoke from the fire was good for your eyes. It smoked all the shit and dirt out of them, he said, and that was what his dad had told him.

---

The next place we ended staying for any length of time was Beckton Road, off the A13. Two more sisters came along then, Linda and Susan. Dad even bought a second trailer to accommodate his growing family.

I was in my element, not yet seven but going to work with Dad each day, knocking on doors and offering to asphalt people's drives, or trim hedges and trees. We made a decent living as we pushed out further and further into Essex and beyond.

Dad didn't read, and neither did I, so the road signs meant nothing to us at all. Still, we knew our way about better than most. Us travelling folk have a great sense of direction and once we've been down a road, we never forget it. We remember every hedgerow, every house, every farm. When we were in the country, there was a series of signs us gypsies left for each other to signify things like: 'This farmer is all right – pull on here' or 'Farmer a right bastard – don't bother'. Most farmers were okay in those days about us pulling on to their land, and if they treated us with respect, we repaid them by doing a bit of collar and treating their land with respect in turn. Gypsies were the perfect employees for the farmers. All cash. No trade unions. We grafted, especially if we were being paid by the amount of fruit we picked, and we disappeared out of their lives when it was finished.

When people started to get a bit lairy with us in the '60s and '70s and kept moving us on, we had to change our tactics a bit. If three or four families moved on to a bit of land, they'd get pushed around by the police, by officials and sometimes by local residents, so we started to pull on places in our hundreds. That way they had to tread a bit more carefully, and it took longer for them to get all the court orders necessary to move us on. It's natural, really: if a group of people or a race is picked on, they seek safety in numbers.

Life in the vardo was good. There wasn't much room, but we knew no different. The space in the gorger houses, and the distance people sat apart from one another in their armchairs, puzzled us. Some gorger families even sat in separate rooms! A big family with Mum in the kitchen, Dad in the lounge, Johnny in his bedroom and Jenny in hers. Weird.

We sat and watched the telly like other families; *Coronation Street* was a favourite. I don't remember any storyline about travellers pulling onto a bit of land behind the Rover's Return, but we liked it. The only programme I can recall seeing gypsies in was an episode of the kids' programme *Black Beauty*. I enjoyed it because I liked horses, and there were plenty of scenes of rolling green fields and that sleek, shiny black horse cantering around to alert the father that the daughter was in trouble. That particular episode had Alan Lake in it, the man who married Diana Dors and then shot himself, and he played a particularly nasty piece of work who was, you guessed it, a gypsy. Problem was, whatever programme or film we watched, we would reach the climax and the generator would conk out. That always seemed to happen.

Christmas was great. We always had a tree and put decorations up, but we didn't send cards to each other. Never could see the sense in that. Most of us couldn't write or read, and why send a card to someone you are sitting opposite from, who you can just say 'Happy Christmas' to?

Wally got a cushty Chopper bike one year. They were all the rage – all the gorger kids sped around town on them – but Wally didn't seem to know what he had. Before New Year's Day, the thing was smashed to bits and left to rust behind the trailer.

All the men went to the Boxing Day racing at Sandown or Kempton, and if I was lucky, sometimes I could tag along. They drank in the bars below the stands, moving out every 40 minutes to place a bet and watch the race. Sometimes they just watched the little telly thing downstairs and didn't even go out on to the course, they were so engrossed in their drinking.

I was seven when I blagged my first job. Dad and me were tarmacking a drive and I got a bit bored as Dad was finishing up the work. I wandered down the tree-lined road, inspecting the state of the neighbouring driveways. One had cracked concrete like streaks of lightning leading up to the front door. As bold as brass, I stood on tiptoe and rang the bell.

'Hello, mister,' I said, going straight into the spiel I had heard so many times. 'Would you allow me to give you a good price for ash felting your drive? We're only working across the road, sir, and I can see your drive is cracking.' The man looked down on me with a friendly smile. My confidence rose. 'Our price is reasonable, I can promise you that, sir, and we does a good job for you.'

'And what is your reasonable price, young man?'

I rubbed my fingers on my chin, looked down at the drive and walked up and down it, just like I'd seen the old man do a thousand times. 'Eighteen pound. We can do it for £18,' I announced, after pretending to be deep in thought for some seconds.

'Done,' said the house owner. 'That sounds like a very reasonable price indeed.'

Just as I was making the arrangements to start, Dad wandered over.

'I'm just telling the man we can do his drive for £18, Dad,' I told him proudly. Dad rubbed his chin with his fingers and walked up and down the drive.

'I think it might come to a bit more than that,' he said finally.

'I've already agreed a price with the young gentleman,' said the man, 'and if that doesn't stand, I'm not interested.'

Dad said we'd start in the morning. Sitting in the truck on the way home, he told me he was proud of me. I'd never felt so good as I did that day.

The following morning, we drove over to Barking, east of London, to pick up some asphalt. As usual, there were queues of lorries and trucks waiting to drive into the yard to be loaded up by a JCB. Dad kept all his equipment on the back of his TK Openback, but there was always room for a deposit of asphalt. Whilst waiting, travellers from all over would jump out their trucks and stand smoking and catching up on the gossip. We drove back to the man's house and did his drive. He was happy with the job and gave me the £18 when we'd finished. I handed it over to Dad, who peeled off a couple of green one pound notes and tucked them in my shirt.

Back at home, Mum would be busy preparing a meal for us all whilst the girls went into town munging. They'd catch the bus to the nearest shopping centre, their bags full of heather, and then walk around selling it. When they'd finished, they would put their coins together and return home. They didn't do too bad either. It wasn't unusual for them to bring back £30 – a fair amount of money in those days.

Dad and me would be starving when we got back from our hard day's work – all that tarmacking and rubbing our chins. Although we would probably have had a fry-up in a café first thing in the morning, nothing else would pass our lips all day. We'd have a wash outside the trailer if the weather was kind, and then get stuck into Mum's home cooking. It might be bacon or meat pudding, or Joey Grey stew. Quite often, we'd have a rabbit or a hare if we'd been hunting with the dogs the night before, or else one of the boys who was handy with a sling would bring back an old pheasant he'd hit whilst it roosted in a tree as dusk fell. On special occasions, we'd have a hedgehog and then pick the bits of meat from between our teeth with its spikes. Leave off! I'm joking. It's a bit of an old wives' tale, gypsies living on hedgehogs. There isn't enough meat on them for one thing: you'd need about 30 of the fuckers to fill us lot up.

Mum kept the trailer spotless. Our homes were immaculate, sparkling and shining inside and out. She'd spend most of the day cleaning and polishing, washing and ironing. Sometimes she'd send one of the girls out to get water, but normally one of us boys would be chief water-fetcher. Dad would pull into the nearest petrol station and fill up the huge metal churn we carried with us. The water was used for washing, cooking, drinking and keeping the horses and dogs fresh.

Dad's passion was horses. I remember moving site one time and having seven lovely black-and-white mares on the back of the lorry. What a sight that must have been! He wasn't really a horse dealer, but he did buy and sell them as a sideline. His special interest, though, were the horses that had a little man in a coloured, peaked cap on their backs. Dad loved a bet – horses, dogs, cards, spinning the coin, whatever. He'd bet on anything, and I got to know the inside of a betting shop at a very early age. Yet it seemed we never went without, and he always had money to hand over to Mum for food and clothes. We had nice trailers too, Vickers Loomsdale and West Midlands were among those we lived in over the years.

Some of the older travellers scorned us for having such modern homes – many of the older generation had refused to break with tradition, keeping their charming barrel-top wagons, which were still horse-drawn, and not even making use of the generator for power. Instead, their old stoves, fuelled by coal and wood, provided warmth in the winter and were used for cooking. Fixed wooden beds could also be found inside, with space beside them to hang and store clothes. The caravans were often painted in the most amazing colours and designs, and each had a small set of wooden steps leading up to the door.

Ben Moore and his wife Chart were a couple of the old school, good people. When we left a site, they'd pull off last. We'd see them in our mirror at the end of the line, their old horse pulling them along. By the time their horse pulled them in to our next site, it was about a week later, and sometimes we were ready to move on again. But Ben and Chart weren't going to change for anyone.

When the evening meal had been had, us kids would go off and play until it fell dark. The evenings always seemed so long. Some of us would kick a football around, others would spar, a few would tend to the horses. If there was an old factory around, we would have great fun gathering stones and smashing all the windows. Disused factories seemed to be all over the place in those days – there always seemed to be one nearby, wherever we landed. I'm pretty sure they were derelict – they were after we'd been crawling all over them for a few days, at any rate. If we were lucky we'd find some scrap metal inside, or some electric cable, and we'd strip it out and lug it back to the site. We were taught young the value of what most other people thought was junk. We'd struggle home with all sorts of riches: cast-iron gutters and down pipes, heavy old manhole covers, the lot.

One evening, an ice-cream man pulled into the site, in a pink-and-white Mr Whippy van. He must have seen all the kids playing from the road and thought he was on to a winner. Kids equals ice-cream equals money. He parked up, turned on his loudspeaker and played a tune to announce his arrival, then sat back and smiled as thoughts about retiring to Sicily flooded his mind. Within seconds, kids had swarmed all over the van as he leaned out the side window, excitedly taking orders. 'Two 99s for you, young man. A Fab? Yes, here you are, madam. A Mivvi coming up.' As he handed over the ices, the kids ran or just sauntered off. I don't know if the ice-cream man thought some adult was going to appear and pay for the lot, but it took him a while to fall in.

'One at a time,' he shouts, but kids are climbing up at the side window and have opened up the driver's door, and are coming in through there too. They're passing boxes of cornets out to a sea of grubby outstretched hands.

'Get out of my van, fucking animals!' he shouts, his Italian temper flaring, but we all take advantage of the distraction and leap in the serving window.

It's too late. His fridge has been cleared of all the lollies and choc-ices, and even the boxes of flakes have been found and passed outside. A few of the older boys and girls have climbed on the roof of the vehicle and are jumping up and down. 'Get down off my fucking roof!' he shouts as he bangs on the ceiling. There are as many girls in his van as there are boys. In fact, one girl is filling cornets from the whipped tap for the others. He doesn't know what to do.

The man may have lost all his stock but he's not going to lose his assets too, so he climbs over into the driving seat and fiddles at the ignition. 'Who's got my keys? Give me my keys.' I think he's crying, but no one hands over the keys. Everyone is laughing madly instead. Then he jumps out the van and curses us in a language I'd never heard before. 'Keep the fucking van,' is the only bit I catch before he storms off the site. Then the older boys and some of the men appear from inside their trailers and the wheels and tyres are straight off. Someone puts a tube into his tank and sucks out the petrol, spanners appear from nowhere and bits of the engine are dismantled. In no time, all that is left of Mr Whippy is a shell. Even the windows go when we use the van for target practice.

I've seen police pull on to a site and receive a similar welcome. If they weren't pelted with a hail of bricks and stones, they would certainly be distracted as they sat talking to children with angelic faces, while other kids would place nails under their tyres. When they'd sniffed around for long enough and it was time to leave, they soon found they weren't going very far with flat tyres. You'd watch them get all nervous when they had to get out from the safety of their cars and be without their radios in close proximity. We were taught from as soon as we could understand not to trust the gavvers. They were the enemy.

Sometimes after work and a good meal, us boys would be allowed to accompany the men to the pub. We'd all get washed and shaved, put on our best shirts and pressed trousers and give our hair a good comb-up. A lot of landlords would turn us away. No gypsies, they'd say. Some pubs even had signs nailed up. Landlords could tell by the look of us or our voices. We were used to this, but it gave us the hump nevertheless. In their opinion, we were trouble. Sometimes we were, but certainly not as much as the local hooligans, who thought nothing of glassing each other. When a landlord didn't even give us a chance, we'd more often than not tip a pint of beer over his head and move on to the next pub.

If a publican treated us with respect we'd return it, if he didn't we'd be the trouble he expected. I knew many good landlords who knew we just wanted to sit and have a drink and a banter. Most travellers are good spenders too, and some of them knew that. On the occasions when a fight did break out, more often than not it would be us fighting among ourselves, and any damage would be paid for.

There was a man, a gorger called Gratton Puxton, who came on the sites. He was something to do with the National Gypsy Council and was a student-type bloke, a good man, who wanted to give the gypsy children the chance of an education. If they wouldn't come to the schools, he brought the schools to them. He sent double-decker buses in with teachers aboard, and they'd wait for the kids to come and learn. I felt sorry for the well-meaning teachers and for Grattan, because the only people I ever saw on them buses were the teachers.

About this time, the first council-run permanent site was opened in Hainault, Essex. It was a sort of compromise between the authorities and gypsies. It stopped us moving around, but we didn't have to move into a house. These sites were clean, with brick-built communal showers and toilets, but many travellers viewed them with suspicion and saw them as the beginning of the end of a centuries-old tradition of life on the road.

There were good reasons why we travelled. It wasn't just for fun and novelty, or to annoy local residents. The men were not part of the normal workforce. Very few gypsies worked in factories or offices – they couldn't even if they wanted to. We worked on the land, or through our own enterprise. Now, if you're tarmacking drives, or sharpening knives, or cutting back trees, or doing a bit of roofing, you can't keep revisiting the same streets time and time again. Well, you could, but you'd soon find the work dried up. Therefore, every few months you try somewhere new. We were getting on our bikes to find work long before Norman Tebbitt thought of it.

Often, we didn't know where we were going when we left. Dad would drive. He may have memorised a bit of the land he'd clocked on his travels, or he might spot some trailers somewhere and pull over and join them. That's how it worked.

But such things didn't bother me at the time. I just wanted to make my Dad proud, so from the moment I could walk I was learning how to fight. Whilst other toddlers were playing musical chairs or ring-a-ring-o'-roses, I was learning how to keep my guard up. As I got bigger, I began to fight with the other kids who shared the same dream. All me, them and Wally needed to amuse us was an old tattered punch-bag we'd hang from a nearby tree to go to work on.

# 3.

# *SINE DIE*

DAD STARTED ACTING AS my manager and promoter before I'd even slipped on a pair of boxing gloves. I'd had plenty of spars and kids' fights on the sites, but was surprised one day when Dad started arguing with a man named Bill Brazil. Bill had claimed that his nephew, Wally Mitchell – known to everyone as Mucker – would beat me hands-down. Dad shook his head violently. 'No, my Jimmy would beat most kids his age.'

Ten years old, and the next thing I know I'm facing Mucker on a patch of land on the site. Dad and Bill are refereeing, and us boys are going at it hammer and tongs. A crowd gathers around and urges both of us on. I'm not sure why I'm fighting Mucker, but if Dad thinks I should then I am not going to let him down. Defeat does not enter my head. I sense this is different from the tear-ups with other kids. It is about family honour and pride.

Mucker is no mug and catches me early with some good shots to the mouth. Straightaway I'm bleeding around the gums and I swear I can feel bits of skin from Mucker's knuckles between my teeth. But, like me, he's a kid, and his fists are not yet hardened. The blows he is landing are doing as much damage to him as they are to me. I see the pain in his face as his fingers and knuckles start tearing like tissue paper. Having taken a bit of punishment and seeing he's not enjoying himself at all, I set to work on his face.

After a while we are both tired and come in close together, heads down. Mucker raises his head. I see he has burst into tears of frustration and he tries to headbutt me. Dad and Bill jump in and pull us apart. I am declared the winner, Dad lifting my little arm in the air.

It was not a matter of shame for a boy to burst into tears when he'd had enough. We were too young to know about the niceties of the bare-knuckle ring – saying 'I've had enough' or 'I've given best' – and were not yet powerful enough to spark each other. I was amazed afterwards when told that our bout had lasted just under an hour. That spoke volumes about our fitness and stamina as kids, and well, time flies when you're enjoying yourself.

Shortly after that, I was put up against another boy called Freddie Bradley. Freddie could have a fight all right, and we were much more evenly matched. One fight I would win, then the next Freddie would take, and others were draws. Our fights always drew a small crowd and I learned a great deal from them. I started to learn about pacing yourself, about soaking up punishment and about knowing your opponent. Most importantly, I learned how to take defeat. Freddie and I became great pals.

My brother Wally, although 18 months my junior, was also beginning to make a name for himself as a young fighter. I remember a time when we'd pulled up on a bit of land near Kempton racecourse and Cliff Ingram, the grandfather of the Frankham boys (Bobby, Jimmy, Tommy and Sammy) challenged my Dad to let Wally fight his Jimmy. The Stockins and the Frankhams go back years. Both are fighting families, but through the generations we've always been close and I have the greatest respect for them. Johnny Frankham, who became the number five light-heavyweight in the world, is one of the most decent men I know.

Back to the fight. accuse me of bias, but Wally at 11 years old still looked like a boy, while Jimmy Frankham was a lump for his age and more like a youth. The fight was arranged, with gloves to be worn, halfway up the lane that led to the site. I always remember Dad, Wally and me walking one way down the lane and the Frankhams with old Cliff Ingram in tow coming the other way. *High Noon.* It was agreed that the fight would be three two-minute rounds, and that Cliff would referee.

---

Wally starts well. He's always had speed, and plants a flurry to Jimmy's head and body. The bigger boy comes storming back and backs Wally up, catching him with some solid shots. Wally keeps his guard up high and takes a lot of the punches on the gloves. But Jimmy's running the fight, and he's peppering Wally continually. We could do with a break, but Grandad ain't looked at his watch. This is the longest two minutes I've ever seen and it must feel like hours for poor Wally.

Eventually, Cliff calls a halt to round one and Jimmy has taken it. He should have done, with all that time. I thought the advantage rule was only played in football.

The second round is all Wally, right from the off. Employing everything he knows, he switches from head to body and back. Jimmy tries to hold him close, but Wally is having none of it, springing back and zipping around him, throwing out sharp, accurate punches. Dad and I think Wally might finish it now, but Cliff's called time on the round! Talk about looking after your own. This round has been half the length of the first. 'See fair play now, Cliff,' shouts one of the Pidgley clan who had gathered to watch.

The Pidgleys were a big gypsy family and, in recent years, one of theirs, Tony, has made a huge success for himself as chairman and owner of Berkeley Group, builders of luxury houses. Why he chose to go into houses and not caravans, I don't know. Tony Pidgely can't read or write either, but he hasn't done too bad – I hear he is now worth £60 million. He was the adopted son of Bill and Florence Pidgley, who lived for some time in an abandoned railway carriage near Walton-on-Thames.

Cliff's faulty stopwatch doesn't matter after all, because in the final round Wally's straight on his opponent, and young Jimmy knows that he is in for the kill. A few more searing blows to the head and Jimmy Frankham drops his hands and bursts into tears. End of fight. Wally is the victor. A real case of little boy, big heart.

---

My brother Wally was always getting himself into scraps, but most of them were not of his making. One day he was out in the field pooving the grys when three older local boys ambled up and started to throw stones at Dad's horses.

'Stop that!' shouted Wally across to them. With that, the three boys approached him.

'Make me,' demanded the biggest.

Wally, sensibly, ran off and came and found me. We hatched a plan whereby I would hide behind a bush and Wally would go back and offer all three out, then I would jump out and help him. But they saw me creeping up before we could get to them, and scrambled away to mount their posh Claud Butler racing bikes. Wally managed to grab the mudguard of one as he attempted to ride off and it toppled the boy. With the mudguard in his hand, Wally set about the boy's head.

'Leave me alone, you animal, I shall tell my parents,' cried the boy and we laughed at his silly accent. But we let him go, relatively unharmed, so were therefore quite surprised when one of the men on the site bought a local newspaper a few days later. An article in it told how a single local boy had been ambushed by a 'gang' of gypsies and beaten senseless with his own bicycle.

Whenever we stopped somewhere new, there would always be stuff in the local paper about us. It was normally pictures of the piles of rubbish we had made, although, more often than not, this was scrap which the men had collected and you can be damned sure were going to sell. These pictures were accompanied by stories of cats going missing (I suppose the implication was we were eating them) and other terrible but unsubstantiated crimes.

My first fight wearing gloves was for Kingston Boys Club. I'd been going down there and training for a while, and had been doing quite well. The trainer decided to put me on the bill for a show down at Roehampton. I was fighting another 13-year-old called O'Reilly, and was as pleased as punch when the ref declared me a points winner. Dad was there, as were a number of uncles, and I felt I had acquitted myself well. From that night I had a target. I wanted to become a boxing champion. I knew I had the ability, commitment and courage to become one, but also knew I had to work, work, work at it.

We moved over to Ruislip Boxing Club when our travels took us over that way, and Dad kidded the trainer that he'd lost my medical card, so I got issued with another one. This enabled me to bend the rules and box as often as I liked. The rules then stated that all boys should have at least seven days' rest between bouts but, with my two medical cards, some weeks I boxed two or three times. I would have boxed every night if I could have.

My progress was fast, and I made the Junior ABA finals, staged at the Hilton Hotel in London, and then the NABC finals held at Aldershot. Although I lost on both occasions I was not downhearted, knowing that it was a real achievement to get so far, so quickly. I loved the thrill of boxing and was a willing pupil. With the encouragement and enthusiasm of Dad and Wally, I was determined to turn professional. I could see the future now, and it looked good.

---

I was on a roll, having won my last three or four fights, when I came up against a boy who had been in the ABA championships. I was very confident and when I looked over at him I just knew I could take him out. That is often the way – your instinct tells you whether it is going to be easy or hard. This boy didn't look good. He reminded me of the type of nervous lad who had just left school and would serve you in a men's clothing shop. He didn't look scary, or even hungry to win, but halfway through the first round he landed me with a fast right that I didn't see coming and I hit the canvas. Managing to get to my feet on the count of eight, I looked over at the ref and he nodded for us to box on. My head was just clearing when my opponent almost lifted me off the floor, with a flashing left this time, and I crashed over again. Once more I managed to get to my feet on the count of eight, and avoid any further hits until the bell goes. I walked, light-headed and weak-kneed, over to my stool. 'You're doing well, son,' lied my corner-man.

Seconds out for round two, and I convinced myself things can only get better. Smack. I walked straight into a right-hander and this time I couldn't beat the count. So much for my instincts.

Driving back in Dad's truck, he tried to cheer me up 'He was very good, that boy, it was too early for you, Jim, that's all.'

I wasn't really listening, having noticed a brand-new-looking jacket on the seat next to me. I slipped it on and it fitted perfectly.

'Whose coat is this, Dad?'

'It's yours, Jim. You bought it this afternoon on the way up. Remember?' No, I didn't.

'Where are we stopping, Dad?' I asked after a while.

The old man turned and looked at me strangely. 'Are you all right, son? We're stopping at Sunbury, where we've been for five months.'

I was concussed, but didn't know it. The next day I had a blinding headache, but other than that it was just my pride that was hurt. I became doubly determined to keep training and keep learning, and most importantly never to underestimate anyone again.

---

Like many youths, I got involved in a bit of street fighting during my teens, and I'd be lying if I said I didn't enjoy it. It was all good practice for the real thing and I loved bringing down swaggering bullies a peg or two when they thought that because you didn't have cropped hair and wear army boots, you were a soft touch.

I was no different from other boys in wanting to go out and drink, chat up the girls and have the occasional fight. One such time was when I was in a disco opposite the Spread Eagle pub in Epsom. Trouble couldn't have been further from my mind as I stood and watched the local girls wiggling their bums to the Isley Brothers. At least, that was until Jimmy Adams, a gypsy boy, decided to take a pop at me. Our fight spread outside and Jimmy got hold of my hair, which was long then, and punched my face continuously. Eventually he let go and ran off down the High Street.

In the morning I told Dad what had happened and, with no further ado, we hopped into the motor and drove over to the Beddington Lane site where Jimmy lived. There was no reply when we knocked on his door, but plenty of people clocked our arrival as they pulled back their curtains to have a look.

Within the hour, Jimmy arrived back on our site, driven by his father Teddy Adams. 'Let the boys sort this,' said Dad.

Teddy agreed. The last thing either of them wanted was for them to get fighting, although it has to be said that many fights between travelling men arose from arguments over their kids.

The fight with Jimmy did not last long. I put a flurry of punches on his face and he didn't fire back as I backed him around the ring. Within two minutes, Jimmy gave best and didn't want to carry on. We shook hands and our fathers did the same. Fair dos to Jimmy though, I had moved on a bit in fitness, experience and technique and outclassed him that day, but him and his father came over alone – not mob-handed – and didn't make a mountain out of a molehill.

Another time, I took my sisters to the pictures. I hadn't long had a motor and I was proud to drive them there. Can't remember what film we went to see, but I do remember that the motor conked out on the way back, and I had to get the girls out the car and get them pushing it to give me a bump start. I glimpsed another boy I knew driving past, and I could see he was laughing at the sight of my sisters pushing a clapped-out car down the road, with me sitting uselessly at the wheel. I was fuming, and that night I went to the pub where I knew he would be and bashed him up. I just couldn't get the picture of him laughing at my family out of my mind until I did it.

---

I'd seen what Gypsy Johnny Frankham had achieved in the ring, and I wanted to emulate that. I trained, trained, trained and fought as many bouts as I could. But it was not to be. Just as I was approaching my 18th birthday, something happened that changed the course of my boxing career, and my life, I suppose.

Wally, by now, was an accomplished young boxer and we were both on the same bill for a show over in Ruislip. The trainer of the boy that Wally was to fight approached him and told Wally he had no chance. 'I'm that confident,' said the trainer, 'I'll have a straight £50 with you.' This upset Wally, which I'm sure was the intention, and he stormed off to tell Dad. The old man would have been on a high, settling down to watch his two boys fight in respected amateur bouts, having had a few bottles of Pils lager. What Wally told him incensed him no end. He was a fiery man with a quick, and sometimes dangerous, temper. He collared the trainer outside the dressing-room.

'What's this about a £50 bet?'

'What bet? I don't know what you're talking about.'

Crack. Dad had chinned him, knocking the man to the floor. Meanwhile I entered the ring, not knowing about these developments. Only when I had won the fight and was back in the dressing-room did I hear about what had gone on. Wally had his bout and won, and the three of us set off home.

A few weeks later, we turned up back at Ruislip for another inter-club tournament. On our arrival, we were informed that we have been banned for life from amateur boxing. The official terminology is *sine die* [sin-ay-dee-ay]. In the dictionary it says that this is Latin for 'without fixing a day for future action or meeting'. All three of us were gutted. It was a shock and that term, *sine die*, stays in my head even now. I suppose the amateur boxing officials would have written and told us the bad news had they had somewhere to send the letter to. Kevin Finnegan, one of the famous boxing brothers, was once *sine die* when he leapt into the ring and clumped the referee, following what he thought was a bad decision against his brother Chris.

Of course, we appealed and kept on appealing, but it seemed to fall on deaf ears. The Stockin boys were out of the amateur boxing game.

I couldn't accept that after 180 amateur fights that was it. I continued to train, and volunteered at every opportunity to spar with established boxers, to help in their training for big fights. John Conteh (a gentleman) and Frankie Lucas were among the big names that warmed up on me at various times. I recall a black guy who gave me a hard time. He was a light-heavyweight and I was a light-middle, and he boxed my head off. For three fucking weeks I sparred with him and he took right liberties, knocking shit out of me night after night without so much as a thank you at the end. I didn't really go back into him as best as I could, because in the back of my mind I was still harbouring hopes of getting my licence back, and didn't want to put a foot wrong. I took his arrogant and uncalled-for punishment every afternoon until one day I decided enough was enough.

---

Climbing through the ropes I know today is the day. The smirk on his face when we touch gloves in the middle of the ring makes me even more angry. 'You're cannon fodder, gypsy boy,' says the smirk. Battering time. We exchange some opening punches, but it soon settles into the pattern of the previous spars, with him unloading some big bombs to my head and me attempting to keep his more vicious efforts at bay with my jab. As we come out for the second round, I am ready for him. Backing him up on the ropes, I hit him with everything. All my anger and frustration over my *sine die* status comes exploding out, as well as my basic instinct to teach a bully a lesson. A massive punch up his ribs comes almost from the deck, and he sinks to the floor letting out a loud groan, no longer the cocky bully. 'Get up, you cunt!' I shout as I stand over him. 'I've not said a word for three weeks about you taking the piss. Come on, get up and fight!'

'You hit me low,' he moans through the pain in his ribs and a shattered ego.

'Hit you low – my foot. Everyone in the gym saw that hit. It was a perfectly good body shot. Now get up and fight, instead of making piss-poor excuses.'

He didn't. He wouldn't. I never saw him at the gym again and although he was making a good reputation for himself before, I never came across his name again. He either changed it or retired.

I don't think I ever consciously decided that if I couldn't be a good professional boxer, then I would make sure I was a bloody good bare-knuckle fighter, but things started to drift that way. I don't believe I ever went looking for fights or challenges, but they seemed to follow me. The three stories I'm about to recount are typical of how these things happened, and they all took place shortly after my *sine die* took effect. I don't feel I started any of them but, in each case, I ended up in an unplanned fight.

---

One cold crisp morning, Wally and I are out for our daily run. I'd got out of a warm bed for this and, as usual, Wally is sprinting off ahead. He obviously hadn't drunk as much as me the previous evening. Just ahead are two men walking towards him. As Wally passes, one sticks his elbow out and jars my brother in the ribs. Very strange – two men strolling along here at seven in the morning, and one of them elbowing Wally like that.

'You cunt, what was that for?' Wally cried.

'Don't call me a cunt,' he retorts and they start fighting. Wally does him in a few seconds, and by now I've caught up. I am more baffled than annoyed.

'Why did you do that?' I ask, but he has no answer, just stares at me blankly. Now I am getting annoyed. So I clump him on the jaw and knock him out.

His mate just stands there staring. 'If I hadn't been here, you'd have joined in on my brother, wouldn't you?' I challenge him.

'No, I wouldn't have, honest.' But I'm not listening, and I crack him too. He goes down and lands on top of his mate, who is still out cold.

Wally nudges me. 'Let's jell, bruv, before the gavvers come and we get loud.' Wally and I resume our run, leaving the two weirdos piled on top of each other.

Another night, I'm having a drink in a little back bar in the King William pub in Ewell. It's only a short walk from the site where I am staying, so I use it quite a lot. The clientele is a mixture of student types and local lads, and the pool table in the middle of the back bar is the central attraction.

A young lady comes in the pub, and a lad in my company by the name of Edvard starts calling her names and taking the piss out of her. She nips back into the other bar and gets the boyfriend, who Edvard, if he'd had half a brain, would have realised was there. The boyfriend chases Edvard around the pool table, and he leaps a couple of stairs, bursts out into the car park and sprints off as fast as his legs can carry him. I'm left in the bar, standing there sipping my beer.

The boyfriend doesn't bother chasing Edvard, but comes over and squares up to me. I try to calm things down.

'I've said nothing to your woman, mate. She'll tell you that. So do yourself a favour and leave me out of it.'

'Well, your mate has done a runner, so you'll have to apologise on his behalf.'

All eyes are on us. The pool balls are still. The fruit machine has stopped tinkling and only the jukebox continues to play.

'Have this for an apology.' I smack him clean between the eyes. He goes over, but staggers back to his feet. I see I've cut his eye. I move over and hit him again, and this time he stays down. I nip off quickly, because I know who'll get the nicking if the gavvers turn up. Back on the site, I give Edvard a bollocking and a smack up the earhole for being such a wanker and dropping me in it.

Finally, we are pulled on to a bit of land over at Walton. Twelve-odd trailers, I'd say. It is a sunny Sunday afternoon, about three o'clock. Me and Creamy are leaning against an old van, talking and idling the afternoon away. Walking across the field towards us are two young gorgers. They've got a bit of gold on, earrings, short hair and plenty of tattoos, and look like they are coming for a purpose.

'Who's the best man on here?' asks the bigger of the two mushes, as he breathes lager fumes in my direction.

'What?'

'Who's the best fighter on the site?'

'I don't know,' I reply honestly.

'Well,' carried on the gorger, as if he was explaining the route to Heathrow Airport, 'I've been in the pub with my mates and I've had a bet that I'll take on and beat the best man you've got to offer.'

'Well, mate, I'm not saying I'm the best man, but I'll oblige you.' I call out to Dad, who I think is probably having a doze in the trailer. 'Dad, there's a man out here says he wants to fight me.'

Dad comes out and speaks to the man, who explains again, very politely, about his wager.

'Take them rings off then, bruv,' says Dad, nodding at two or three chunky sovereign rings screwed on to the fella's meaty fingers.

'No, they don't come off,' says the man, shaking his head.

'Fair enough.' Dad smiles and takes off his horseshoe ring and another buckle one and hands them to me to put on.

The man takes his top off and passes it to his mate to hold. As soon as he holds his hands up, I hit the fella two or three times and he's down on his arse with a busted mouth, which is pissing blood. Respect to him though, he hauls himself up and declares, 'I ain't had enough yet, pal,' through bloody, fat lips.

I switch him off good and proper with the next punch. His mate has seen enough and throws his pal's top in the air as he makes a hasty retreat across the field.

'Ain't you going to have some?' shouts Dad after him, laughing loudly.

'No, I fucking ain't,' we hear him reply, as he almost falls over himself in his panic.

A few seconds later, the first man is coming round. Mum leans over him with a pail of water and a towel and helps him clean up. When he gets to his feet, he looks at me, Dad and Creamy one by one, smiles and says, 'Thanks very much. Good to meet you,' and sets off on his way.

# 4.

# SHOW OUT SUNDAY

**EPSOM DOWNS AT THE** time of the annual Derby race meeting is one place where all gypsies, from all over the country, love to be seen. Travellers have been turning up there in their masses for centuries now, so the local council fences off land and, for a change, allows us to pull on. This we used to do in our thousands, forming one huge carpet of chrome on the slope facing the winning post. Sparkling Westmoreland, Eccles and Vickers trailers everywhere.

Friends and cousins who hadn't seen each other for months or years were reunited. It was like one massive family get together. Friendships formed were no less strong because you hadn't seen each other for a while. You might be living as a brother to a boy for six months, and then if your dad decided to move on you didn't see him again for a year or two, but if anything, it made people closer.

Dogs barked and horses grazed, women chatted, the men caught up on all the news and the kids – well, they were in their element.

Small boys would weave in and out of the caravans on little motorbikes, skidding in the mud that the weight of hundreds of trailers had created, or performing daring wheelies on the gravel. Their teenage brothers would drive around the site in their dad's or elder brother's pick-up trucks and one or two of the more reckless would even venture off and take the vehicle down Ashley Road into Epsom town centre.

It was not unusual, during Derby week, to see the top of a kid's head through the driving-side window of a car, and a couple of small hands, with loose gold rings on, gripping the top of the steering wheel. The gavvers turned a blind eye. What could they do? Risk chasing the kid – because he ain't going to be flagged down – and someone getting hurt? Take him up the site and tell his mum and dad? Charge him?

'Name?'

'Smith.'

'Address?'

'No fixed address.'

No. They knew it was our week and that there was no malice in our behaviour, and the bottom line was that they couldn't police us, so there was no real point in being confrontational. I wonder, though, how many bemused policemen have sat in their patrol cars by the old clock tower in Epsom, at the end of a long shift, and have rubbed their eyes on seeing what seems to be a driverless pick-up truck heading in their direction.

While us kids played all day and generally got up to mischief, the men would be gambling with cards or by spinning coins. Fights would be talked about and perhaps arranged. It was inevitable. The other side of the coin of everyone getting together was that old arguments, feuds or threats could resurface.

We'd follow the men to the nearby pubs: the Downs Hotel, later to become the Rubbing House, the Derby Arms, the Amato or the Ladas, and wait until closing time, when sometimes they'd brawl amongst themselves. More often than not, it was forgotten by the morning.

There is an old fable that every year a gypsy creeps to the Amato in the dead of the night before the Derby to write the name of the winner of the big race on a drinking trough or wall outside the pub, and that it is always correct. I don't know about that, but I'm sure that one night as I passed by, I saw the then guvnor of the pub standing outside in his pyjamas with a stick of white chalk in his hand.

Back on the Downs, someone would light a fire and the storytellers would take over: says about bygone Derby meetings, yarns about huge amounts of money won or lost, or how famous jockeys or celebrities had come and celebrated on the camps with us. Other tales would frighten you, excite you or make you laugh. Who needed books when we had the likes of old Uncle Jack, his craggy face illuminated by the flames?

One say that sticks in my mind concerns my cousin Billy Smith's father, Matty. Apparently, he struck up a relationship with a local gorger girl, but there was a snag: her long-standing boyfriend was a Teddy boy who was known as the local hardnut.

In those days all the young people, it seemed, hung around in the local cafés. Teenagers sipped on tea to make it last, and the more flush among them fed the jukebox. It was quiet, the time after the workers have finished their breakfasts and before the first of the lunchtime trade arrived.

Matty was already in there when King Ted barged in, walked straight over to his table and demanded he come out into the street to fight him. They left the café and fought around the corner, in a place not visible from the main road.

The fight went on for an hour, with the spectators having time to pop back to the café for the occasional cup of tea or egg on toast. Both youths were as good as the other, it seemed. Finally, two policemen appeared from across the street and the crowd dispersed. Matty and the Ted stood there cleaning themselves up and tucking their ripped shirts back in their trousers.

'You two lads okay?' asked the first policeman.

'That was the best fight I've ever seen,' said the second officer, 'and a fair one at that.' He pressed a pound note into the Ted's hand and said, 'Now go off and get a drink together.'

Johnny Frankham can tell a good story. One I remember was supposed to have happened to him, but I fancy it's a story that has been passed down the generations, with the names changed to suit the circumstances. Johnny would tell the story in a deadly serious voice, and we'd be all ears, hanging on his every word as the fire crackled and glowed.

Johnny and his brother Sam were driving through Oxford one sunny afternoon when their truck passed a well-dressed young man on a bike. He was wearing a tweed suit and his trouser legs were restrained from flapping by bicycle clips. The cyclist felt that the truck had passed too close to him and began waving his fist and shouting at the brothers.

'We'll have a laugh here with this mush,' smiled Johnny.

They pulled up and the man approached. 'I say, that was damn close to me, I suggest you drive with a bit more care and attention in the future.'

Johnny and his brother started to laugh at the man's indignation and plummy voice.

'It isn't a laughing matter,' protested the man. 'Do you want fisticuffs?'

With this, he held his fists high, John L. Sullivan style.

John and his brother were shocked and amused. Little did the man know that the two were seasoned street fighters, one of whom would one day become a famous boxing champion.

They agreed to step off the road into an adjoining field. 'Now,' the young man lectured as if he were talking to a couple of dunces, 'when I say "commence", we come out fighting. Do you understand? Commence. Commence means start. Remember that word. And we fight on until one of us says "submit". Submit means give in. Do you understand?' He was talking as if Johnny and Sam were subnormal, but they just smiled, knowing that Johnny would soon splatter the young fool.

The man took his jacket and shirt off and neatly folded them up. As he came to the middle Johnny took a swipe, but the young man ducked and bobbed up with an uppercut, and put Johnny Frankham, future boxing champion, straight on his arse. Sam was puzzled. Johnny was puzzled. He got up, and the man danced around him and managed to get through his guard again, putting Johnny straight back on the deck.

By now Johnny was dazed, and the man spun him round and crashed a blow into the side of his head. Johnny was back down for a third time.

Sam was worried. Johnny Frankham was taking a beating. This went on for about a quarter of an hour. There was blood now on Johnny's face, but somehow he managed to catch the young man with a combination which had him on his knees. 'Submit!' shouted the young man before Johnny could advance any further.

'That's it! Sub-mit. I've been trying to think of that fucking word for the last ten minutes,' gasps Johnny.

It doesn't sound so funny when I repeat it like this, but try to picture Johnny's deadly serious tone, and us all around the fire listening to this respected man telling us how a skinny gorger toff gave him a beating, only realising at the end that it's a wind-up. We fell about laughing.

The Derby is run on the Wednesday and the Oaks, the big race for fillies, takes place on the Saturday, or they used to anyway. For some reason, they've changed the Derby to a Saturday, and it has never been the same since. It makes me sad when I watch it on the telly now, and it only looks a little busier than normal race days. In the old days, from the rails back to the starting post, it was heaving with people and caravans: now, you can see huge swathes of green and empty patches.

Derby Day was a national holiday for the common people and was an institution for rich and poor alike. Now, it is little more than any other big Saturday meeting. It is very sad, and I cannot see any logic for changing it.

Derby Day itself had a special magic. Everyone seemed to be in high spirits and were well disposed to each other, with the exception of one or two bare-knuckle fighters.

Characters like Prince Monolulu, an exotically dressed man, who weaved among the crowds selling his tip for the big race, and the bible bashers, were part of the atmosphere. The bible bashers were showmen in their own right, standing on an upturned crate and drawing in a crowd with their dire warnings about drink, gambling and other vices – the very reasons most of the crowd were there in the first place.

Our own gypsy women would have their best day of the year at the

Derby as they accosted the drunk and merry, with offers of telling their fortunes from a crystal ball or reading their palms. Of course, this was a load of old cobblers, but if it made people happy and our ladies could take a few quid, then who's complaining? If our womenfolk really possessed a special power that enabled them to see the future, then I would have consulted them before I fought Creamy.

But perhaps the biggest day of all for us was the Sunday before the big race, when a huge market takes place alongside the racecourse. Stalls selling everything fill the Downs, and the crowds are huge. We call this day Show Out Sunday and it is exactly that – a chance to show out and show off. Mum and Dad would put on their best clobber, and me and Wally would be washed, scrubbed and dressed up to the nines. The girls would be on parade in their best, colourful dresses, with their hair tied up in ribbons. We would all look stunning: 'Look at my boy, ain't he grown big?' and 'Look at my girls, ain't they a picture?'

The best china would be out on display inside the trailer, visible through the windows, because the lace curtains would be drawn back. The trailers themselves would be gleaming, the polished-up chrome reflecting the sun.

We'd walk off the site and head down in groups to the dip where the market had been set up. Across the road, up on Tattenham Corner, you could see and hear the sound of the funfair kicking into life. Thousands of people would already be descending on the market. Travellers who were now living in houses came to soak up the atmosphere. Black people, Asians, Chinese, gorgers of every sort turned up to see what they could buy. For us it was a carnival, your birthday and Christmas rolled into one.

Mum would look around the china stalls and check out the price of the Crown Derby, standing out with its gold-rimmed edges amongst all the shit. 'How much is that, mush?' gypsy women would demand from the man running the stall. Whatever price he said, they would gasp and feign disinterest. 'Look, mush, that's too dear, and youse knows it. I'll give you . . .' And so began the bargaining process.

If we're buying, we like to haggle and will rarely buy anything at a quoted price. Of course, these traders know that and they know we love the old Crown Derby, so they set their prices higher and act all annoyed when they finally hand over the piece to the likes of my mum, for 'Bugger all – don't you tell no one now, luv, will ya?' hoping that she'll tell everyone she sees. Mum's happy – she's knocked the bloke down, and he's happy – he's moving his stock.

Gypsies have to feel they've got the better part of any deal with the gorgers, even when we are selling rather than buying. If we're selling a service, we'll always start with a ridiculously high price, knowing that the punter will knock us down, because he's been brought up to believe that we will try and rip him off. When we settle we'll still be making a reasonable profit, and he feels that he's checked our greedy instinct.

It is all a game and normally both sides of the transaction know it, but it goes wrong now and then. You quote someone £500 for a £250 job and wait for the negotiation, but they say 'Yes – go ahead.' What would you do?

We used to stop and watch the con men who auctioned goods from the back of a lorry (this helped convince the punters they really were getting a bargain) with well-rehearsed and clever patter. 'Who'll give me £5 for what I have in this box?' the man would shout. An unconvinced crowd would remain silent.

'Don't you trust me, girls and boys?'

Finally, a lady would step forward and offer up her blue note. 'Clever lady. Here you are, madam,' and then he would gleefully rip open the box. 'You've just bought yourself a £300 dinner service for five measly pounds.' The crowd would gasp and the lady beam as the man passed down the set to her. Some time later, being one of the team, she would return the set to the back of the lorry.

Meanwhile, the young Arthur Daley would be motoring away. 'Still don't trust me, boys and girls? How much do you want to pay for these toasters?'

We'd watch admiringly as the men whipped the punters up into a frenzy, increasing their audience by the minute until, in a climax of greed and panic, they'd empty half the contents of the lorry at prices which were by no means bargains, leaving the crafty cockneys with a tidy and legal profit.

As young kids, we terrorised many of the conventional stallholders. Twenty of us would pick our moment and flood a stall. 'How much for them earphones, mate? Them ones up the top.'

'I'll give you a quid for this,' picking up a car radio.

''Ere, bruv, I bought this last year and it don't work,' flourishing an old torch.

The market man would be like a goalkeeper trying to defend his goal, turning to face first one of us and then the other. Meanwhile, others would be grabbing what they could and disappearing into the crowd. He'd know it was a sting but, although cursing us, rarely laid a finger on us or gave chase. One, he wouldn't want to give us further pillaging opportunities, and two, one of us might get our dad. Behind the stalls, they'd have fierce Dobermann or Rottweiler dogs tied up to their Mercedes vans to stop any of us attacking from the rear.

When I was older and talked to some of these guys, I realised that they regarded the pilfering as a sort of tax which they couldn't avoid, but did try to minimise. This tax was worth it to them, because for many of them the Derby Sunday market was their biggest day of the year, when they could take more money than they ever dreamed of. Pitches were much prized.

When we were teenagers, though, Show Out Sunday meant more than the market and the fair. It meant girls. Gangs of boys would walk around in their finery and girls did likewise. We never looked twice at gorger girls and the gypsy girls didn't even glance at the gorger boys. You'd try and catch the eye of a girl you fancied and if she looked interested, you'd keep an eye out for the future.

Towards the end of the afternoon, we'd leave the market and walk around the fair. Many of the travellers went in for the greased-back hair, the Elvis look, set off with yellow-coloured dealer boots, but that was never my scene. I wasn't mad about Elvis, although many gypsies were. I liked lots of music, though, especially country and western and, a bit later, Bob Marley.

Gorger kids would be everywhere in their gangs, but they left us alone and we did the same. Although we were similar ages, probably looking for the same thing, it was like two different worlds. Mind you, we couldn't resist winding them up sometimes. Always you'd get a big gorger boy showing off to his mates or girlfriend by punching a medicine ball and getting a high score for strength, or trying to make the bell ring by bringing down a big hammer on a spring. We'd send in the least likely looking one of our number, maybe a kid three years younger than the gorger, to follow straightaway and make his effort look pathetic.

The boxing booths were gone by now, which was a shame. We'd heard so many stories from Dad and the others about what could go on inside. Freddie Mills, the British boxing champion, was said to have started his career in the booths at the fairs around Hampshire.

Dad always made sure we had money for the fair and Show Out Sunday. He'd store up a bit of scrap metal for a couple of months beforehand and then cash it all in. This would take care of his beer money, some cash for Mum and pocket money for me, Wally and the girls.

As soon as we hit our teens, we'd be allowed to go with Dad and the other men to the pub and join in the card schools or the pitch and toss. Even in those days, a thousand pounds could ride on a simple game of heads or tails. Large wads would change hands under the table in the blink of a fat old landlord's eye. Not that they would have bothered. At times like this, our money was as good as anyone else's. Sometimes, the Old Bill showed their faces in the pubs. Their presence was meant to be more of a deterrent, really, than a harassment. I suppose they thought that if we knew they were in the vicinity, we'd be less likely to turn to brawling.

One Derby week, I didn't make it. I was banged up in Ashford Remand Centre for driving on a ban. A fella called across the bar to my Dad: 'Hey, Muggy, who's the best young fighter around?'

'My Jimmy would take some beating,' Dad calls back.

'Go and get him then, I'll fight him and beat him,' announces the man, Bill Smith, who was well known to the family. He probably knew I was unavailable and had decided to wind Dad up a bit.

Dad, as you've probably gathered by now, didn't take a lot of winding up. 'I can't get Jimmy right now. But if you really want a fight, why not try my other boy, Wally? He's younger and smaller than my Jim, but he's scared of no man and will give you a good fight.'

Fight on. A crowd gathered outside the pub as Wally, all of 17, stripped to the waist and started to limber up. Bill Smith did the same. He was full of beer and the dangerous self-belief that comes with it. In some ways he couldn't win. If he beat Wally he'd be accused of being a bully, but if he lost he'd be taunted about being beaten by a boy.

If Wally lost he'd lose no face – as a boy, he would be seen as brave for trying, but Dad might have looked bad for putting his boy's name up.

Boxer Tom, a much-respected former fighting man, was quickly roped in to referee the match and see that fair play was upheld. He called the man and boy together and the fight started. Racegoers hurried away from the paddock to join the growing crowd. Women practically ran over, holding their floppy colourful hats on their heads, their high heels sticking in the mud. Beer tents emptied as the bush telegraph worked at its fastest speed. It was all to no avail, though, as Wally let rip with half a dozen sizzling punches. Fight over. Bill Smith switched off.

One year Wally had a bright idea. He was going to make a few bob, he said, and he nipped back to the site from the Downs, fetched some tarpaulin and poles and erected a tent of sorts. He scratched the word 'Toilets' on a piece of card, sat outside and waited to take money.

There's always a shortage of toilets on Epsom Downs during Derby week, and within seconds Wally had his first customers. A bunch of drunken lads dismounted from an open-topped bus and filed straight in to Wally's tent, paying him 10p each for the privilege. They weren't bothered that there were no actual toilets inside, and just sprayed the contents of their bladders over the good old Epsom turf.

Then two posh ladies turned up. Wally thought they could have been royalty, or at least that's what they say now the story has been embroidered over the years. They exclaimed, 'Thank heavens. A lavatory at last!'

Handing Wally their ten pence pieces, they trod gingerly into the tent before the sight of 12 red-faced young men energetically shaking the drips from their coreys sent them screaming out of the tent. 'I should have charged you double!' shouted Wally after them, as they ran away hollering about fetching a policeman.

---

A few years later during Derby week, Wally was to feature in one of the famous classic fights. It all started so unexpectedly. He got into an argument with a man over pitch and toss. He didn't know the man from Adam, but carried on arguing because he felt strongly that he was in the right and that the man was not being straight. It was all over a £5 note, but the two men were shouting in each other's faces, and it was obvious that a fight would have to be had. 'Fight me!' screamed the man, his veins nearly exploding in his neck.

Within seconds they face each other in the gambling ring, people scooping up coins around them and scrambling out of the way. It seems that within a minute, half the people on the Downs know a fight is off. They jump up on to car roofs, giving their mates a hand up to get a better view. They don't care if the motors get dented – they're not their cars. Revellers clamber up to the top deck of the open-top buses to look down, and the rest push and shove to try to get a better vantage point. 'Hold tight, Miranda,' shouts a toff as he pulls his girlfriend nearer the action.

Wally hasn't got a clue who he is fighting, but a man behind tells me it is Johnny Docherty. Straightaway, I know the name. He's an Irish traveller with a big name for bare-knuckle fighting, and he's so good he's about to turn pro as a boxer. In short, Johnny Docherty was famous. I wasn't sure if it was a good or a bad thing that Wally didn't know the reputation of his opponent.

The first ten minutes go by with both men evenly matched and landing crunching shots to one each other's heads. Each hit is marked by a cheer from the crowd. They are so engrossed they fail to notice that the first of the afternoon's races is off behind them.

Then Wally seems to move up a gear, delivering crisp punches and literally running rings around his opponent. The more Wally speeds up, the more Johnny slows down.

The crowd senses that the Irishman is in retreat, and they urge Wally on for the kill. He lands a stinging jab into Johnny's already swollen eye, and I see him wince with the pain. 'Go on, Wally boy, you've got him!' I scream, but he can't hear me above the din.

Wally is moving in on the Irishman and a flurry of blows sends him reeling backwards. Johnny responds by trying to kick out at Wally as his balance falters. Wally positions himself and lets loose the lot: jabs, hooks, rights and lefts. A complete box of tricks. The Irishman drops his hands and sinks to his knees. The fight is over.

The two men shake hands and Johnny Docherty says something about seeing Wally next year. The crowd cheers and claps, having been entertained far more than they had imagined. Some of the more enthusiastic do more damage to cars as they jump off the roofs and down on to the bonnets, rushing to congratulate both fighters. They know and I know that we'd seen a pretty special bout: 20 minutes of furious yet clever boxing. No poncing about.

It's a bout that fighting people and gypsies still talk about now. Someone even made a video of the fight, which has been in circulation ever since, although I only got to see it in recent years. It confirmed that the fight was everything my memory told me it was.

The police turn up and fight their way through the crowd, but no one really makes a gangway for them. The racegoers don't want to see anyone nicked, especially the two men who have just fought so bravely and put on such a show for them. 'Why don't you fuck off and mind your own business?' says a man in a suit and top hat. 'Go and arrest that Geoff Lewis, he's the real criminal around here,' joked another man who had obviously lost his money on the jockey's mount in the first race.

I don't know what Wally would have done had he known it was

Johnny Docherty he was fighting. There was no doubt that Wally was the better man on the day, but if he had known, he may have given unnecessary respect to the man and undermined his chances. Wally won because he wasn't fighting a name or a reputation, he was fighting a man he was furious with.

There was never any rematch and I didn't hear of Johnny Docherty ever turning professional, but I could be wrong. He is certainly a well-respected man in travelling circles. As for Wally, even though I knew he was one tough fella from hours and hours of sparring together, I realised that day just how *good* a fighter he was. One of the best.

Years and years later, Wally and I had reason to make ourselves scarce and we pulled on some land down at Bognor on the south coast. Adjoining the land was a yard with a house and more than one Rolls-Royce was parked outside. We had no money, and Wally put his apron on and started to make us both up some Joey Grey. There was a knock at the door. 'We're from next door. Like to come for a drink?'

We didn't know the men, but recognised them to be travellers. Travellers who had obviously done well for themselves.

'We're skint,' said Wally.

'Don't be silly. It's on us. We know who you are. You're Wally Stockins. I saw you fight Johnny Docherty on the Downs years ago. Great fight.'

---

Other fairs and festivals we visited regularly were Stow, down in the West Country, Doncaster, Barnet and the famous Appleby Horse Fair. Many of the fairs and shows have gone now, and more are being shut each year – not because they are no longer economically viable, but because local communities object to the annual 'invasion' of gypsies.

It's a great shame, for these fairs have been a place for generations where extended gypsy families can meet up and new families can begin. Many a gypsy couple began their courtship at one of these fairs.

They were important for the continuance of our culture, and they have also been part and parcel of rural life in England for centuries.

Horsmenden was another event where us travellers congregated every year. This was held deep in the heart of the Kent countryside, on the second Sunday of the hop-picking season. Gypsies and gorgers all converged on the small village green, and the same stallholders that you'd see on Show Out Sunday would be spread all over, selling their wares. Boys could be seen riding bare-back on horses around the green, or controlling a huge horse with just a piece of rope slung around the animal's neck.

Ponies and traps trotted along the road. Men and boys sparred out on the green and the pubs sold lots and lots of ale. Add a few fire-eaters and you've got Merrie England in the Middle Ages.

The fair's history is associated with hop-picking, and the tradition of the poor people of London and the gypsies traipsing down to the hop fields of Kent every year for their paid holiday.

It was here, as a teenager, that I got into an argument with a gypsy man by the name of Chonker. He told me I was a stupid, lippy 16-year-old. He may have been right, but that was no reason for a big 40-year-old man to crack me on the jaw. Instinctively, and before I knew what I had done, I laid one back on him and, like a big old oak tree, he toppled to the floor. He was spark out and it was some minutes before his eyes started flickering and he slowly climbed to his feet. I was ready to keep him going down, for I didn't fancy another right-hander from the bloke. 'I don't want to fight you, boy,' Chonker said.

The next day, as we collected the wages from our little bit of hop-picking, Chonker ambled over, took my hand and clasped it tightly in both of his. 'No hard feelings, Jim.' I nodded in agreement. 'That was the hardest punch I've ever taken from man or boy.'

Chonker was gracious in defeat. It can't have been easy, being laid out by a boy. But in most cases, fights between gypsies were had and that was it. There were rarely any grudges held over, or escalations of the violence. Fighting increased our regard for each other, not the other way around.

Fights were conducted fairly. Challenges were not thrown out to people who clearly couldn't or didn't want to fight. People didn't get knifed or kicked in the head when they were down, which can be the way with others. It had to be that way. We had our own code by which we lived, and by and large it worked. We looked out for our children. We didn't steal from one each other. We respected our old folk. Looked after our women.

However, when we fell out with people outside our immediate community, we found that sometimes they played by different rules.

5.

# GUIDING LIGHT

**BEING BANNED FROM AMATEUR** boxing didn't stop me and Wally training, Wally especially. He worked and worked and eventually decided he wanted to try his luck at a few pro gyms. He obviously made an impression, because he caught the eye of George Francis, the man who had trained many good boxers, most famously Frank Bruno. George told us he saw a lot of himself in Wally, and that he had fought bare-knuckle before turning to gloves and finally carving a name for himself as a top trainer.

Wally settled in well and became friendly with a lot of the seasoned pros. Cornelius Boza-Edwards, a world champion in his own right, sparred with an eager and raw Wally, and my brother soon decided he wanted to get back into the ring as a pro. *Sine die* didn't apply to professional boxing.

When I say that boxing and fighting was in our blood it is true. Our grandfather, Dad's father, Wally, was a boxer who fought 13 times as a professional, and Dad's five brothers, Rymer, Joe, Amos, Dido Bill and Jukebox, were all fighters. By all accounts Rymer was the most talented, but Jukebox had the best name. Uncle Jukebox. And you know what? I never thought to ask why he was called that.

Dad made his name in, and earned his living from, the boxing booths as a young man. Once a familiar sight in fairgrounds up and down the country, they are extinct now, although I can remember seeing them as a kid. Dad would stand outside the booth stripped to the waist and looking the part, whilst the showman would gather a crowd around.

The showmen were the people that ran the fairgrounds and, like the Romanies, for centuries they had travelled around the country, taking their fairs from one town to the next. They owned the rides and the sideshows, and these attractions would be passed down from father to son.

The Matthews family was probably the best-known show people clan. Show people don't like being called gypsies and we don't like being confused with show people, although we share some common language and the trait of travelling.

As Dad stood outside the booth, a plant in the crowd would mouth off and shout that Dad was no fighter and he'd teach him a trick or two. The showman would pretend to ignore him whilst the plant pretended to become more and more angry. Eventually, the showman would accept the man's challenge on Dad's behalf, and a hungry and swelling crowd would move with them inside the tent, shelling out florins to the cashier on the way in.

Joe Public would then jump in the ring and him and the old man would have a seemingly hard fight, which Dad would edge. The showman would then flourish his white fiver and say, 'This is for any man that can knock him out.' The local hardmen, on seeing how close the last man got and now almost in a frenzy, practically fought each other to be the next man in.

Very rarely did Dad lose, and his payment was £3 per fight, plus the nobbins tossed into the ring by an appreciative crowd. After a really good fight the nobbins could amount to the same again or more. It was a good living, because Dad sometimes had ten or 12 fights a night. Fifty pounds for a night's work in the 1950s was big money but, of course, the fairs only ran in the summer months, and not every day by any means. And for a job where sometimes you have to be almost carried home, you'd want £50 a night.

I remember Dad telling me how he and Mum had only been courting for a short time when he persuaded her to come and watch him in the booth. He shaped up to fight the first oncomer, and could feel his shorts were loose and, to his horror, were slipping down his waist. He had nothing but a pair of swinging bollocks underneath, so to save his embarrassment, and Mum's, he let the man's first punch knock him clean on his arse. The punch, Dad said, was like a flick from a little finger, but the man went off thinking it was the easiest £5 he ever earned.

Mum and Dad went from strength to strength, eventually jumping the broomstick at Epsom Downs and eloping. Dad was 24 years of age when they married and the first thing he told Mum he would do was retire from the boxing booth. She insisted there were easier ways to earn a living.

Mum told me that when they got back from eloping they were cold and hungry, and pulled up outside a little café in Rose Hill. Dad couldn't decipher the menu, but Mum could read a bit. They just made out the words 'Welsh Rabbit'. Father was starving. 'I could do with a nice bit of rabbit,' he said as his stomach rumbled, but his face dropped when he was served up a piece of cheese on toast instead of a fat old bunny.

The family was full of characters, and Rymer was the most colourful one of all. What Rymer didn't do in his life wasn't worth doing. Stories about him were the stuff of legend. Although Rymer was still very much alive when we were kids, it was the says they told about him around the fire that really captivated us all.

Freddie Mills and the white fiver story was one we loved to hear time and time again. Like Dad after him, Rymer was a fairground booth boxer, and possibly the best one in the country for a while. One of his young contemporaries was Freddie Mills, who was turning heads in booths across southern England. The two young men met and knew each other, as two people in the same line of work do.

Both turned professional boxers at about the same time. Rymer assumed the fighting name of Jack Daly. He had an incredibly good run of ten fights and ten wins, all at the Winter Gardens, Bournemouth, and it wasn't long before he was scheduled to fight Freddie Mills, as he himself moved swiftly towards becoming middleweight champion of the world. The match was billed at the Winter Gardens in 1939, but was unfortunately postponed indefinitely when an altogether bigger fight disrupted everything. Hitler was throwing his weight around and picking on people who couldn't fight back.

Rymer's professional career lost its momentum in the war years, and soon he was back in the boxing booth earning money the hard way. Years later, when Freddie's fighting career was ending and he had become a television celebrity on shows like *What's My Line?*, he spotted Rymer, who was stopping at Littleton Lane near Shepperton Studios. Freddie was making a film and was being driven to the set. He ordered his chauffeur to pull over, and jumped out and greeted Rymer like the old friend he was. 'How you doing, Jack? This your boy?' Freddie picked up young Wally, Rymer's boy, and held him aloft 'This little bruiser will be the next champion of the world.' From his wallet he pulled out a white fiver and pressed it into the boy's hand.

I'd like to add the romantic postscript that the Freddie Mills white fiver stayed in the family to this day, but the chances are that Rymer had laid the money on a horse before Freddie's Rolls-Royce had turned out of Littleton Lane.

Freddie had asked Rymer to spar with him and help him get fit for a comeback fight, I think for a light-heavyweight title against Gus someone, but it didn't help – Freddie lost. Although his connection to the family was slight, Rymer and his brothers were upset when Freddie shot himself in his car not too many years after that.

People who knew Dad after his boxing booth days remember him for his love of horses and gambling. He really did love it. He loved winning, and he loved losing. Sounds ridiculous, but it's true. He wasn't one of those blokes who sulk or get violent or drunk when they lose. He just smiled and carried on with his business, as he would when he won. I've seen him win five grand and I've seen him lose five grand. Both times he kept the same expression on his face.

Many times I've stood there as Dad has gambled £100 with another man over who can throw a penny nearest to a wall without hitting it. It would be all he had in his pocket sometimes, but if he lost he smiled, paid the other man with no bitterness, and went on with his day.

Of course, he liked it a bit better if he won, and one of my happiest memories is of him, Wally and I at Lingfield when we went through the card. We came home from that course with our pockets bulging with £20,000 between us.

Wally threw the wrong ticket away that day, and when he went to collect on the last race, the bookmaker tried not to pay him out. As they argued, the bookie started to pack away his things. 'Look, mate, you ain't got a ticket and I didn't take your bet,' he insisted.

Dad and I fetched the course adjudicator, but there wasn't much he could do without the ticket. Then I noticed Wally throwing sideways glances at another bookmaker behind, who was hurriedly stuffing his gear into a big leather bag. 'Hang on a minute. It was you that took my bet, wasn't it?' The bookie couldn't have looked guiltier if he was caught stealing the notes from Wally's pocket. If the racecourse man hadn't of been there, and he hadn't paid up so readily, we'd have given the man a beating for trying to fiddle us out of a lot of money.

Wally was with Dad once when he was still quite young and the two of them had to go to Hull to get the truck repaired. Dad had saved up and had finally put together a nice wad, and was going to get the truck back into good working condition.

Getting there in the early hours of the morning, they slept in the cab to gone midday and then got up for a walk through the town and to find some scran. But before they found a nice café, Dad spotted a bookmaker's, and with no opportunity for Wally to guide him past, he was in there. Wally's heart sunk as Dad peeled off two fifties from his wad. The old man couldn't read much, but he knew the words 'Lester' and 'Piggott', and he could copy the name of his mount on to a betting slip.

Despite the urgings of various old codgers in the shop shouting 'Go on, Lester', Lester didn't go on. Wally winced as Dad doubled up and pulled four fifties from his roll of notes. He went up to the *Sporting Life* page tacked to the wall and ran his finger down the runners of the next race until he found L. Piggott. This time, Lester didn't even get up with the front runners.

Wally tugged on Dad's arm, but he just smiled his 'don't worry, son' smile. Wally could see them heading back down south in a still-broken and unreliable TK Max, a grand lighter. Dad put £400 on the third race and searched out Lester's name again. This time, our man hit out at the front from the second they left the stalls, and even though everyone around him was jumping up and down and mentally counting their winnings as Piggott opened a bigger and bigger gap, Dad remained calm, with the same kind smile on his face. Lester's horse came in at 3–1, and Dad was in profit. Collecting his winnings at the glass counter, he turned to a relieved Wally and laughed: 'Now we can get a really decent job done!'

I didn't really like Dad gambling and if I was with him I would normally try to keep him away from the betting shop. But as I got older, I realised that it wasn't a problem. He just enjoyed it. Why shouldn't he do something that gave him pleasure?

I like a game of cards or coins and the occasional bet, but I've never really considered myself to be a gambler. Mind you, I did win a trailer off a man called Scouse once over the flick of a coin. It was worth £2,000 then, and I picked it up off him the very next morning and sold it that afternoon. Scouse had another trailer, so I wasn't leaving the man homeless. I would have done, though, because it had been a fair bet, and I know that if he had won he would have taken mine.

Dad's gambling was real because we saw it with our own eyes all of our lives, but old Rymer's heroic gambling exploits were family legends. As I said earlier, you could earn big money in the boxing booths if you could last out, and Rymer as a young man saw plenty go through his hands. In 1938, he laid £1,100 to win £1,000, a huge amount of money in those days – probably two to three years' wages for the average working man. The horse lost, too, beaten into second by a judge's ruling. There were no photo-finishes at that time.

His really big bet, though, was in 1956, when Rymer rocked the bookmakers for so much money they thought it was a syndicate at work. It started almost as a whim. He had befriended a German man, who had decided to stay in the country after the war following a period of internment as a prisoner of war. The man raved about the German goalkeeper Bert Trautmann, who was playing for Manchester City. 'He will make that team win the Cup,' he predicted earnestly.

Rymer was always a man to see fate in things and proceeded to back them round by round as they progressed. With each victory, his conviction became stronger and stronger and his stake bigger and bigger.

By the time Man City reached the FA Cup final against Birmingham City, Rymer was a rich man, but with what he intended to stake on the final match, if Manchester won he'd be £22,000 in profit.

Joe, his brother, who was shrewd with money and later became a millionaire in his own right, tried to persuade Rymer to back Birmingham. He pointed out that that way he couldn't lose. But Rymer was having none of it. He was on a path and was determined to see it through to the end. Rymer, Joe and his boy Aaron even went to Wembley on two tickets. The other two squeezed young Aaron through the turnstile between them, and cheered Manchester City on to a 3–1 victory, and Rymer to £22,000 in cash.

Poor Bert Trautmann, though, the seed of the bet, broke his neck in the game, but knowing that Rymer had so much at stake, carried on playing to the end of the match.

I don't know what 22 grand would be worth at today's money. Somewhere between half a million and a million, maybe. Whatever, it didn't change Rymer's life. He made sure of that by spending every penny. He bought some land and scattered a few new cars around friends and family, but the rest went back to where it came from in no time: the bookies who cried so much when Rymer took it from them in the first place.

Through his professional and fairground fighting, Rymer came into contact with all sorts of people and inevitably met up with the gangsters of the time. He sometimes had drinks with Jack 'Spot' Comer and a man called Johnny Rice, whom he always spoke highly of.

Comer was the so-called King of the Underworld for a time in the '50s, before Billy Hill and, later, the Kray twins. Rymer said he was a Jewish man who had earned a lot of respect among people for standing up to Oswald Mosley's Blackshirts when they were stirring up racial hatred in the East End of London in the 1930s.

A funny story Rymer told was how his name was put up to get heavy with someone somewhere who was owed money and wouldn't pay. They wanted Rymer to apply some pressure, and were willing to pay him £100 for the job.

The client drove Rymer to the victim's house and, after pointing it out, Rymer started to get out the car with a starting handle he pulled from a holdall. 'What do you want that for?' asked the client nervously.

'When I do a job I like to do it proper,' explained Rymer.

'No, no. I only wanted him to be frightened,' exclaimed the man.

He became so anxious over what Rymer might do, and for his part Rymer played it up as much as he could, that the client ended up paying him £150 to forget the whole thing.

---

Meanwhile, going forward a couple of generations, with Wally now pro, I find myself fighting in the less formal environment of a family party. I'm in a pub in Romford, celebrating the birthday of another travelling man, when Northy Danny comes over and accuses me of nicking his young brother's burger off the bar where a bit of a spread had been laid out for the guests.

I tried to laugh it off, but Danny was having none of it and insisted on making a scene. I couldn't work out why. I had had a few fights by now, and word gets around I suppose. Maybe people took me to be a fighting man and some of them felt a compulsion to pick a row. Surely he couldn't really be that upset over me picking up the wrong bit of chuck – even if I did?

To get it over and done with I planted one on his chin, but before he could retaliate or I could follow up, a bunch of people had stood between us. 'I'll see you in the morning,' I promised as I left the party, where I had the funny feeling I was no longer welcome.

'That's fine with me,' growled Northy Danny.

We were pulled on at Palmer's Farm, and the next morning I was up at the sparrow's fart, strolled across to his trailer and rapped on the door. There would be no 'Good morning, my friend', and I didn't think Danny was about to invite me in for a little pot of tea for two.

He bustled straight out and we went to work. I was a better fighter than him and within a minute he dropped his hands and said he'd had enough. I think now he believes that I didn't chore his brother's burger.

---

Back in the gym, I got to sparring with Frankie Lucas, who was in training for an upcoming British title fight with Tony Sibson. He had been a good amateur, having been trained at the Sir Philip Game Club in Croydon by Freddie Rix, who is Clinton Mackenzie's father-in-law.

I sparred with the man for three weeks and he was one tough fighter. He didn't hold back, and tested my chin to the limit. I was sure sometimes he wanted to knock me out, which wasn't really in the plan, but it was a challenge and made me spar better. He was a strong half-caste fella, with a Jackson Five-style haircut.

At the end of the three weeks, after the run-up to a big fight, it was the done thing to weigh on your sparring partner with a few quid, or at least a couple of tickets for the fight. Frankie came across with fuck-all.

When I sparred with John Conteh, on the other hand, I found him to be a thoroughly nice person. He'd been light-heavyweight champion of the world, but controversially had lost his title to Matthew Said Muhamed, who was called Matt Franklin before the Muslim bug hit him like it had other more famous black American boxers in the past. The controversy was over some gooey tar used to repair Matt's damaged eye during the fight.

I don't think John Conteh ever regained his title, but I do recall him fighting a Jesse and an Ivy afterwards. Not two girls he pulled in a nightclub, but Jesse Burnett and Ivy Brown, two hot black American boxers.

I toyed with the idea of turning pro, but Wally had gone ahead and done it. He made his debut as a lightweight and won, and in his next fight he drew. He threw himself further into his training, and he was more than happy with how it was going with George Francis.

George told him one day that he had a third fight lined up, and that if he came to the gym he would be able to let him know where it was and how to get there. This was on a Wednesday morning, and me and Wally went along to the regular horse and general market that was held in Southall, West London. Dad wanted to go this day because he had an old motor he wanted to out and we tagged along with him.

All the usual faces were at the market, looking at the various shapes and sizes of the horses and it was the usual busy hive of activity. The sun was shining and the song 'Ring My Bell' blared out from the traders' radios. People greeted each other and exchanged banter. It was a normal, laid-back market day, and none of us had anything more on our minds other than Wally's upcoming bout and Dad selling his old van.

Dad spotted a man he had had a bit of a wager with. There was nothing unusual in that, because Dad bet on everything and anything with anyone. This one was over a game of pool, where the man had ended up owing Dad £40. 'You flush, mate, to weigh me on that bit of wedge?' asked Dad in a reasonably friendly manner. The man denied owing the money. In fact, he denied all knowledge of any debt at all.

I could see the colour rising in Dad's face. 'Best pay me Dad what you owes him, mate,' I said, hoping to defuse the situation.

The funeral of Janie, Dad's sister, who drowned in the Thames at Richmond in 1945. Dad is next to his Mum, Rymer is on the far right. The grief on their faces is distressing even now.

The girls get ready to go munging in Southend in the 1950s.

Wally leads Dad's horses on Epsom Downs in 1968.

In the trailer.
Dad, Mum, me
and the girls.

Me, Linda, Betsy and Wally outside one of the old boxing booths.

Me aged eight, holding Dad's hand at Auntie Lovey's funeral.

On the road. Mum and Dad with the girls. Wally and I are on the bonnet and Rymer kneels in front.

Wally after boxing for England against the USA.

Wally in action, Johnny Crisp looks on.

Wally shows off Johnny Frankham's Lonsdale belt.

The beer tent on Epsom Downs, Derby Day. From L to R: Uncle Jukebox, Jim Frankham, Cousin Mary, Finney's Frank, Wally (shaping up), Dad, Bill Brown, Joe Mitchell, me, Dido's Jack, Dido's Bill and Aaron.

Me shaping up in 1976. We won't mention the togs!

Sparring with Wally, who was a pro boxer at the time, shortly before the Kenny Symes fight. Look at my belly!

Me with Bill Brown and Finney's Frank, six weeks after the fight with Johnny Love. My black eyes had still not gone down!

A friendly bare-knuckle fight outside the White Lion in Maidstone, 1976. Willie Cole on the left shapes up to Sam Frankham. Johnny Frankham is the fair play man. Dad and I look on. Sadly, Willie is no longer with us.

Mum's family, the Marneys. The man partly obscured at the back is Jim Marney, who fled Ireland after killing a Black and Tan during the Troubles.

'I don't owe him anything, pal, and I don't give a fuck about you,' said the man, turning to fix his eye on me.

I stuck one straight on his chin and he came flying back into me. A crowd quickly gathered around us and the man's brother pushed through and joined in the ruck. For some seconds, it was two on one with a massive crowd around us. The whole market had formed a circle, but Wally dived in and took the brother out with a couple of searing shots and he spun round dizzily into the enthralled crowd. As he regained his feet, he tried to snatch Kenzer Gumble's heavy old walking stick, a wooden, knobbled thing that would have hurt across the nut, but Wally stopped him in time and chased him into the throng.

Meanwhile, I'm still pounding the first bloke and he's done good and proper. He's taken a beating. 'Gavvers coming!' warns someone in the crowd and everything is back to normal.

Horses are run up and down for the benefit of potential buyers as the RSPCA men look on, stallholders shout out for custom and the punters resume business. The fight is already history, it seems.

'Take Wally up the gym, son, and find out where his fight is,' Dad tells me.

'What about them fellas, Dad, they might come back.' I was worried that if they did, Dad would be alone.

'Jim, just go. Give Wally a spar up the gym. I'll be fine. I'm going to have a bet anyway. If they do come back, I'll be in the betting shop.'

Reluctantly, we went, but it is not just with hindsight that I say I had a bad feeling. I wasn't sure what it was, but something made me feel uneasy. We had been in this sort of situation before, but I felt that these chavvies might not let it lie. But Dad was the boss and we didn't argue – ever. Never questioned his judgement.

'Go on – off you go. Give me a chance to nick a few quid on the horses,' and he winked and smiled his wide lovely smile at us.

At the gym, Wally was told his fight was scheduled for the next night at Dudley. We didn't hang around for the spar, but rushed back to the market to tell Dad and plan the little family trip up to the West

Midlands. The beer would flow for sure if Wally won his third pro contest.

As we parked the car and approached the entrance to the market, I realised the sun had gone in, the skies were grey and there was a sheet of light rain falling. Then I saw that the whole market was cordoned off by blue-and-white police ribbons. My stomach turned. Straightaway I saw Dad's coat lying there on the concrete, and next to it was a sheet covering a body.

For a second or two, Wally and I were frozen to the spot. In those seconds our lives changed for ever. Suddenly, we were both grabbed from behind and literally dragged across the road to Southall police station, where we were thrown into a cell. Only when we demanded to know what was going on and the gavvers realised it was our father lying there dead on the concrete did their attitudes soften.

Dad had gone to the betting shop for the afternoon, and at some point had decided to wander back over to the market, to check whether the old van he had for sale had sold or not. Maybe he was in need of a few more quid for one last bet. As he passed the market office, he was waylaid by a group of men. One of them pulled a hammer and struck Dad with all his might on his head.

The single blow killed him. The men piled into a car and made off. Hours later, the car was found burnt out.

The next few hours and days are a haze of rage and utter desolation. However, because we knew without doubt that Dad wouldn't have wanted it any other way, Wally decided to go ahead and fight the mush in Dudley. We both knew that Dad lived for our fighting careers and wouldn't want anything to scupper them, especially now that Wally looked like breaking through.

At the fight, I told the organisers and the announcer about what had happened the previous day. 'Are you sure you want to go ahead?' one of the officials asked me. When I said we did, he asked if he should announce it before or after the fight. I told him to announce it afterwards as it wouldn't be fair to burden the other fella with that information.

Wally fought well, and felt he won the close bout, but the other man was declared a points winner. The announcer then told the crowd over the microphone about the tragic events of yesterday and Wally received the warmest ovation I can remember. Dad would have been so proud of him. For the first time since the cowardly murder, the tears welled up inside.

There was no time yet to mourn or even come to terms with what happened to Dad, because we set straight off to search out our dear father's attackers. We looked everywhere and let it be known that Dad's murder would be avenged, but before we could dish out the justice that we knew, they knew and everyone else knew we would, two of the men gave themselves up to the police.

Dad's funeral must have been one of the biggest that has ever been held. Everyone who knew Dad turned up, as well as plenty that didn't. At times like this the travelling community do their own proud, and hundreds of people paid their respects as Muggy Stockins was laid to rest over in Hanwell.

One of the things that most gorgers seem to know about gypsies is that we burn the home of a man who has died. It is a tradition which, like many traveller traditions, is dying out. Neighbours on your average council estate wouldn't take too kindly to the adjoining house being burnt to the ground, for one thing. But many families do still burn the man's trailer, if he has one. The feeling is that no one wants to see the dead person's clothes and belongings with anyone else. The man's possessions should go with him.

It is also a tradition that the body is brought back to the family trailer for a few days as people come to pay their respects. We didn't burn Dad's trailer because it was Mum's as well and we didn't want to, but me and Wally torched his old truck and stood there with Mum and the girls remembering the man we all loved completely as the flames licked the sky.

Shortly after Dad's funeral, the utter misery set in. I cannot describe how I felt. It's bad enough to lose a parent in any circumstances, but to have the man who had always been your life ripped away in this violent way was unbearable. He was a fighting man and a fiery man, but he was a good man.

In travelling circles, fighting is what many men do. His life was not unusual in that respect. It is not a case of live by the sword, die by the sword. He never killed anyone. He never bullied anyone. He didn't deserve to die in the violent way he did.

My mother was destroyed and she has never loved another man since. My sisters were crushed, and me and Wally were empty and angry. We loved and adored him, and the thought of not seeing his smiling face or hearing his laugh again, was worse than any pain that any human could have inflicted on us.

I knew I would explode with rage and hurt at what these cunts had done to me and my family. Why didn't they wait for me and Wally? It was us they had the problem with. Why didn't we go against Dad for the first time and stay with him? If only we hadn't gone to the market. If only we hadn't had the fight, this wouldn't have happened. If only we could turn the clock back a couple of days. It was all 'if onlys'. But we couldn't change a thing.

It got worse. The men were released on bail, only six weeks after they had been remanded in custody. Who gets bail for murder, I ask you? That was a new one on me. It was a sign of what was to come.

By the time the trial comes up at the Old Bailey, Wally and me are well and truly off the rails and are unable to attend. It was a good job we couldn't, because the two men charged with the murder are found to have no case to answer. No one can believe it. Not guilty of murder. Not guilty of manslaughter. Not guilty of fuck-all. Not even guilty of possessing an offensive weapon.

A man is slain in cold blood with a hammer, in broad daylight and the murderers give themselves up – yet they are acquitted. The trial was a shambles, and everyone knew it. Dad was painted as a person who wasn't nice, and the defendants as coming from good families.

They even brought up Dad's breaking a man's jaw some 20 years earlier. Much was made of his fighting past and his temperament, but the real reason he didn't get justice was because he was a gypsy. There is no getting away from it. Say it had been the market manager that had been murderously attacked with a hammer that day, whether or not there had been a fight earlier. Do you think those men would have walked? Of course not.

Gypsy life is cheap. Gypsies live outside so-called normal society, so they cannot expect to benefit from the justice system. Gypsies don't count.

6.

# ALL THE RAGE

**I WAS BITTER ABOUT DAD'S MURDER** and the court case. Still am. It sent me on a bender that lasted some years. Before then I don't think I had much hate in me, but afterwards I certainly did. Fighting helped get it out.

Sometimes those men getting off with killing my father got me thinking about the prejudices against gypsies. We are aware from the day we are born that we are different. No, that's wrong – we are aware from the day we are born that gorgers are different. We make no real effort to please the gorgers, but the hatred of gypsies I've seen from some quarters I find hard to understand. Have gypsies ever tried to invade Poland? Have they ever tried to overthrow a regime or a monarchy? How many gypsy serial killers have you heard of? How many jobs have gypsies taken from traditional Englanders?

So what is it? We don't live in houses? Maybe. We weren't here from the beginning – who was? We're dirty? Have you ever been in a gypsy caravan? We're rough? Yes, we are – but that doesn't necessarily mean we're bad. We're criminals? I'd be surprised if the percentage of gypsies with criminal convictions is higher than that of any other ethnic group.

We're scroungers? Not until we were forced to stay in one place, and were deprived of making our traditional living, which depended on mobility, did gypsies avail themselves of the benefits system. In fact, gypsies rarely turned to the state for help at all. We were born at home with a relative acting as midwife, we rarely used the schools, we looked after our own sick and disabled and cared for our own elderly people within the family. I have personally claimed dole for one week in my entire life.

Okay, so our lifestyle may be different. Our values may be different, but does this warrant a situation where they don't want us to stop, but they don't want us to travel either?

I'm not into politics. Most gypsies don't care. (Perhaps that's what society does not like – travellers don't want or need others.) It is normally gorgers who take up the fight for us. But I think that only when gypsies denounce their culture, set free their horses, burn their caravans and go to school, will attitudes change. Why are we the only ethnic group expected to do this? I don't see anyone telling Sikhs to rip off their turbans, West Indians to stop listening to reggae or Jews to eat pork.

Because the traditional prejudices against gypsies don't stand up in this more politically correct age, a new tack has been taken in the war against us. Yes – we're not real Romanies. That's the one. Even the current Home Secretary, Jack Straw, drew a distinction between 'those who masquerade as travellers or gypsies and real Romanies'.

This is a school of thought that has been building up for some years, long before New Age travellers and tree people came along. So, suddenly, 'real' Romanies are acceptable. But the problem is that unless you have two dangly earrings, a dancing bear tied up outside your barrel-topped caravan and walk around bumping into things because you're busy staring into that crystal ball, then Jack and his gang don't accept you are a Romany. Of course I'm a real Romany. If I'm not that, what am I? I'd like to know, I really would.

There you go. That's my tuppence worth.

I wonder if the Home Secretary has now decided that traditional Romany sports and pastimes are okay? Although bare-knuckle fighting is arguably the most famous of the gypsy sports, for obvious reasons not everyone can or wishes to participate in it. There are other pastimes that the travelling community has traditionally enjoyed. These include trotting matches, chicken fighting and hare coursing. All are probably illegal, and many people find them abhorrent, but they do happen and are part of the gypsy culture, so I will tell you a little about them.

My view, for the record, is that chicken or cockfighting is cruel. It is something I have never been involved in. Trotting matches are no crueller nor more humane than conventional horseracing. In fact, an animal is more likely to be injured or lose its life in a National Hunt race than it is in a trotting match.

Hare coursing is a blood sport, there is no doubt about that. If you abhor blood sports, then you abhor hare coursing. It is now highly illegal, and severe prison sentences have been dished out to people caught indulging in it. Foxhunting, stag hunting and grouse shooting are no less barbaric, yet you don't go to prison for them. Yet. Wouldn't have anything to do with the different social classes that enjoy these sports, would it?

All sorts of horses can compete in a trotting match, from a pony to a half-bred to a full-bred. They have to be trained like any other racehorse, and be made accustomed to running with the spinner, from which the man steers tethered to them. It is a sort of pony-and-trap race, except that when the animals are in full flight, and the rider is standing or sitting in his tin trap (known as a sulky or a spinner), hair blowing in the wind, you might think you have stepped into a scene from *Ben Hur*.

The horses are traded at such fairs as Appleby, Barnet or Stow, and good racers have been known to change hands for up to £100,000, although you are more likely to pay a couple of grand for a good-looking one-year-old.

Races can be between two, three or four contestants, but normally two men compete against one each other. The distance might be three or four miles for half-bred horses, but will likely be between one and one and a half miles for full-breds.

The two horse owners will have had a large bet between them and this is how they hope to recoup their investment in their animal. I have known of straight £20,000 bets between contestants and, of course, a fair old crowd is likely to have gathered, who will be betting between them in more moderate amounts.

There are favourite stretches of road, and even motorway, where the travellers like to hold the races, and to avoid the nuisance of cars or commercial vehicles, the races are often held in the very early hours. Some councils have even had their own signs made up and erected, indicating that it is illegal to pony-and-trap race on certain favoured sections of road. You could take this to mean that it is fine to do so elsewhere.

As a very young man, I remember going to a trotting match down Portsmouth way with Boxer Tom who, like Johnny Frankham and old Jimmy Frankham before him, was a trolley man. There was a dispute over which pony had won. Our horse hit the winning mark first, but the other bloke just kept going. He said that the first post was a marker, not the winning post. The bloke started screaming at Boxer Tom and his mates started to crowd around him, so Wally switched one off and I switched off another. They paid up then and we cleared off home.

Many, many years later I was forced to dredge up what I thought had been a very insignificant episode from my memory.

Chicken fighting, or cockfighting as gorgers know it, has been around for centuries. Cockfighting is, in fact, the more accurate name, as although hens will fight, it is normally cocks who are put up against each other in the ring. Birds are bred for the sole purpose of fighting: black reds, bantams and duck wings being among the favoured breeds.

The birds are trained carefully, by throwing them in the air to strengthen their wings and by pushing down on their bodies so the bird reacts by pushing upward. It is a form of press-up, you could say, and builds the bird's muscles up. Finally, you present the chicken with a mirror, where it will perfect its technique and learn aggression by attacking its own reflection. By the time he meets the real thing, the cock is raring to go.

Two good fighting birds might lock beaks for as long as half an hour and a fight is won when one bird is killed or runs away. Matches between the bigger birds will not last as long. To be fair, most bouts are won when one bird turns and runs from the other, passing a line that has been drawn behind each bird. Sometimes, a bird will run but change its mind, turn round and come back to fight some more.

It is possible for a top bird to have as many as 20 fights in a career, although by that time the chances are it'll be looking pretty battered, and more than likely will have lost an eye. I've seen a bird which has finally killed its opponent hop up on to the defeated bird's prostrate body and start crowing like it's shouting, 'I'm the daddy, I'm the daddy.'

What sustains the sport is the gambling. These days, a good bird can cost up to £1,500, but the real money changes hands in spectator bets. I remember Johnny Love, the top Kent fighter, paying £600 for a bird, and he's been dead 12 or 13 years now. Sadly, the bird performed badly on its first outing and John wrung its neck. Kent in southern England is the British capital of chicken fighting, although there are still some strongholds in the north.

Because of the sport's illegality, matches are held behind closed doors. Because of the patronage of local people, many of them in positions of responsibility such as magistrates, doctors and policemen, they are rarely disturbed.

Occasionally, nasty-looking spurs are fitted on to the fighting birds, although I am told this practice is now becoming much rarer. I used to wonder who made these spurs. What factory made these implements which could only be for one thing? Or was it some chap in his back garden? Maybe they were imported from some Far Eastern country, where the sport still survives in the open.

Hare coursing is by far the most popular sport enjoyed by the travelling community, although its fans are not restricted to gypsies by any means. Events will attract crowds of several hundred, which is a large number considering the illegal status of the sport. Famous breeders and owners in this underground pastime are as well known as the Aga Khan or Henry Cecil are in flat racing.

Favoured venues for events are Salisbury Plain, Newmarket Heath, Newbury and various spots in East Anglia.

The dogs used are mainly lurchers, a greyhound-saluki cross. The greyhound, or the whippet, provides the speed, and the saluki provides the stamina needed. It works on the basis of one dog, one hare. The hare is set off and the dog follows some seconds later. It might take the dog five seconds to catch and kill the hare; it might take it five minutes.

Half the time the hare, being a clever animal, will give the dog the slip completely. When the dog gets the hare it doesn't rip it to shreds, but shakes it in its mouth like a rag doll, which normally kills it. Usually the hares will be taken home for someone's pot.

Most of the time, a dog will run three hares and the opponent's dog will run three. The dog with the most kills out of the three is the victor. As ever, large amounts of money are staked by the dog owners and the spectators on the outcome.

Feelings can run high at these events, and not so long ago there was a case of a farmer shooting a lurcher dog that was hunting on his land. The young boy who was with the lurcher complained to his father – a travelling man – who went to take issue with the farmer. The farmer then shot the man dead, too. He got off with it as well, claiming self-defence. How an armed man can claim self-defence against an unarmed man baffles me, but then I gave up trying to find logic in the laws of this land many years ago.

---

It was a normal Thursday night in the new, improved Bath Tavern. Us gypsy boys were drinking with the local herberts. I remembered the old Bath Tavern – the Blood Bath – and I cast my mind back to when I lived here in the first years of my life. Twenty-storey tower blocks which keep the sun out and cast a permanent shadow now dominate the place. The grass doesn't really grow anymore. There is just a yellow stain where our site was. The local football team has seized on this bit of land, and they play their matches on a dogshit-ridden pitch.

Some of these families that were with us then have taken council houses and flats and stayed. There are a lot of old travelling families around Mitcham. Unfairly, perhaps, the term 'Mitcham Gypsy' is sometimes used to describe people who want, or pretend, to be gypsies.

Lager is flowing this evening. Some of the boys are drinking from cans with pictures of Page Three girls on them. The jukebox is blaring and, through a haze of alcohol and cigarette smoke, I see a familiar face come through the door and head in my direction.

I'd not seen much of him since the fight with Creamy, but he still looked the same. Kenny Symes had always been a fit man, and had been a well-regarded bare-knuckle fighter for as long as I can remember. That's why I knew it was serious the day Creamy turned up with him. He was famous for having recently felled three men, one after the other – Albert Hughes, Billy Ward and another man were taken on and all beaten by Kenny in the same gruelling session. By now, he was a legend in the travelling and fighting world.

'Stockins – I want to see you Sunday morning for a fight. If you don't want to fight me, then you'll have to pay me £400,' he announced.

'I'll be there,' I laughed, unsure whether or not to take him seriously. If this was Kenny's latest business venture, it wasn't a very sound one. Kenny then looks at Barry Baker and Nicky Deighton, who I'm drinking with, and tells them the same – he wants us all over at Streatham Vale on Sunday morning, but if the others don't want to fight him, they've only got to pay £200. Kenny then turns and leaves the pub.

We look at each other, laugh at the strange episode and get back to the drinking.

On the Saturday night before the fight, I finished up the evening by standing on a table doing a striptease in the White Hart, after a long pub crawl following a lunchtime drink that continued nearly to midnight. I was so pissed it was a wonder I could climb up on the table.

When the pubs shut, it was all back to a squat one of the boys had acquired in a block of flats opposite the Bath Tavern for a blow, and I slept where I finally fell.

Drinking is my life now. That and a bit of puff now and then to mellow me out. The training has gone out the window, and I'm on one big piss-up since Dad died. The anger and despair eats away inside me, and the drink blots it out. It stops me thinking about Dad and how he died. I'm now drinking and fighting and generally being a nuisance.

It was a bad time, although then I thought I was enjoying myself. Letting my hair down. Really, I was mourning and feeling sorry for my own self. Wally was just the same – drinking and fighting, getting in trouble with the law. The two of us were careering towards I don't know what. The lifestyle and lack of training had certainly spread my waistline, and for the first time I had a beer gut and had hit 17 stone.

In the morning, I awake to a tapping noise. I try to ignore it and bury my head deep in the pillow, because I've got a pulsating hangover. Tap, tap tap. Then bang-fucking-bang! Wally never did have much patience. He's shouting through the letterbox now: 'Jim, Jim, are you in there?'

The light is flooding through a chink in the old curtain and I lift my tired and alcohol-sodden body out the bed. For a minute, I don't know what day it is, or where I am.

'Open the fucking door, Jim,' shouts Wally through the letterbox. When I pull it open and wince at the full glare of the sunlight, he laughs at me.

'State of you. Got a hangover, bruv?'

I just nod at him. Talking is too much for the minute, so I just let him follow me back down the hallway.

'You forgetting something, Jim?'

I didn't say I'd work, did I? I hope not.

'You're fighting Kenny Symes in half an hour, or has that slipped your mind?'

I had forgotten. I'd forgotten everything. When you're on the piss big time, you tend to. Days and nights all blur into one. Arrangements, if they are made, are rarely adhered to.

It wouldn't take me long to get ready. I went into the bathroom, cocked my head into the basin and turned the cold tap on. No luxury showers here in Bath Tavern Villas. The water ran through my hair and dripped down my back as I stood up straight. I began to wake up. I caught my reflection in the mirror and didn't like what I saw. I was fat and out of condition, and about to fight a top man. But I wasn't worried, because I didn't care.

I was full of anger and it would be good to have a fight and get some of it out. If Kenny Symes beat me to a pulp, so what? Who cared? I didn't. But why had Kenny challenged me to a fight? What was his motive for laying down the gauntlet? Definitely not the £400, because he knew that I wouldn't pay that, or any amount, to avoid the hassle of fighting him.

Maybe he thought I'd got too big for my boots and needed taking down a peg or two. Since Dad died, I'd not been behaving too well. I had let myself go. Perhaps he thought I was there for the taking. He must have known I'd be no pushover though, having seen me fight Creamy at close quarters. Working out why Kenny Symes wanted to fight me now played on my mind more than actually fighting him.

I jumped into Wally's old Escort van and we drove ten minutes across town to the site we'd arranged to fight at. There would be no men in suits and bow ties, sitting at tables sipping wine and chomping steak whilst they watched us knock shit out of each other, like some of the bouts me and Wally had had as kids at the big hotels.

Once, I saw Randy Frankham fight at a hotel. He lost the first round but came back and won the second and third. The audience loved his youthful spirit and had a whip round. Randy got about £300 that day, and I remember Dad saying that he would have been thrilled with a tenner of nobbins in the old boxing booths.

The crowd today would be rough and ready, and waiting to see what should be a classic bare-knuckle fight. But I was astounded when it suddenly hit me that all the motors lining the roads outside and leading up to the site belonged to people here to watch us. Mercedes, BMWs and Porsches stood out among the trucks, the vans and the Ford Cortinas and Granadas.

The crowd parted to let me and Wally through at the entrance to the site. I nodded at some familiar and friendly faces, but noticed some hostile stares too. I'd walked this walk before as just over a year earlier I had fought Creamy in the same place. Mark Ripley was here again too, and I knew he'd see fair play.

The fair play man in a bare-knuckle fight has a very crucial role. He is entitled to wade in should one of the fighters cheat or be out of order in any way. I suppose that marks prize-fighting out from other fighting sports, in that the ref is entitled, and sometimes forced, to steam into one of the combatants. That is why the fair play man has to be someone who is not only well respected, but can do the business should he need to.

It happens. The fair play man says to a fighter, 'Okay, mate, that was below the belt, now ease up,' and the fella turns around and says, 'Get fucked.' The fair play man takes his shirt off, the other fighter steps out of the ring, and he mullers the other mush. I've seen it.

---

Kenny comes pushing through the crowd towards me and without further ado we square up. This time, I am determined not to take an early severe blow like I did against Creamy. We start slowly, feeling one each other out. He catches me with a good body shot and I am conscious of how much it has slowed me up. He couldn't miss the purr as it hangs like a small sack of coal over my tracksuit bottoms.

The crowd cheers him on, but I'm happy with the way I'm fighting behind my jab. This goes on for a while, and I'm actually enjoying myself. My jabs to his face are having a cumulative effect and his eyes are swelling a bit and his cheeks reddening. Then I start allowing him to come to me and then letting three or four punches go in a cluster around his head. Close up, I can hear that he's breathing heavy. Mind you, so am I.

Unlike with other fights, I've got no game plan. I'm not pacing myself, nor am I moving in for a kill. I'm just playing it by ear. I still don't give a fuck.

Johnny Love (far right) with his father and uncle. Johnny was a good fighter and a good man.

Hop picking in Goudhurst, Kent 1950s. From L to R Dad's cousin Joe, brothers Dido, Amos and Dad.

Cousin Joe and me sparring. Joe is a professional golfer these days. Neville Smith, a pro boxer, stands behind.

Cousin Joe in action.

**Neville Smith, on the left, died suddenly and tragically the day after this photo was taken.**

**Me, Wally and punchbag, watched by a budgie.**

Me and Wally in the trailer.

A real motley crew, especially the man on the far right – one of my co-authors, Martin King. Billy Smith is on my left.

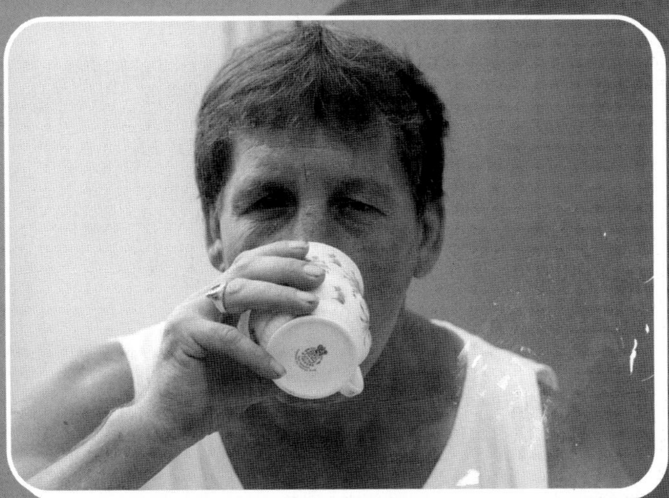

A nice cup of Rosie Lee!

Neville Smith's funeral.

Me, Wally and our boys, by Dad's side.

Dad's grave. He was nicknamed Muggy because as a child he couldn't say 'Mummy'.

The Smiths and the Stockins at the Mansion Lane site.

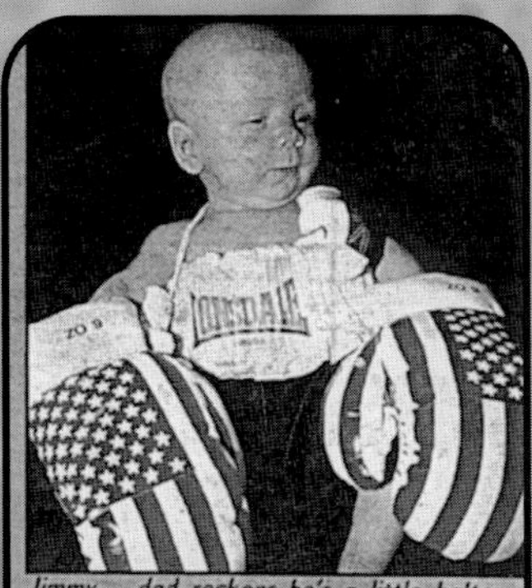



Jimmy . . dad reckons he's a little belter

KID GLOVES
£50,000 on tot to be champ

BOXER Jim Smith will scoop a £50,000 bet if his six-week-old lad becomes a fight champ.

Ex-amateur Jim, 35, is so convinced junior will do the business that he placed the £50 wager even BEFORE the tot was born.

His son is being christened Jimmy Dean Rocky Marciano, after the Forties heavyweight legend who inspired the Rocky films.

Roofer Jim, of West Drayton, Middlesex, who also has three daughters, said: "I'll start training him as soon as he can walk."

Jimmy must win a British professional title at any weight by age 25 to land dad's 1,000-to-1 bet.

Piece in *The Sun*, after I placed my bet on Jimmy Dean Rocky Marciano to become a boxing champion.

Mum sets off for the opera.

The family today. From L to R: Betty, Louie, me, Wally, Linda and Susie.

We both dish out similar punishment to each other for a good half-hour then, as he moves in again, he drops his guard slightly and I release a right-hander that catches him just below the jawbone where it meets the throat. It hurts him bad. I've been caught just on that spot before and know how painful it can be. He can't disguise the pain. 'You all right, Kenny?' asks Mark Ripley as he signals for me to hold off for a second. Kenny nods unconvincingly and we go back to work.

Now is the time to take advantage of his obvious discomfort and I go on the offensive. I summon up all my energy and just hope I don't fuck myself over.

Left and right hooks, uppercuts, jabs machine-gun his face. I'm in charge, taking the piss now. I might be on the drink, but I'm not past it. I'm angry with him now for the first time for challenging me over nothing, so I drop my arms and stick my chin out. Point to it to wind Kenny up. A proper little Cassius Clay.

Kenny takes some free shots, five, maybe, but he doesn't even rock me. Wally's shouting at me for being such a prat. 'Stop showboating, bruv, and knock the man down,' he roars. A man in the crowd tells Wally to shut his mouth. Wally glares at him and for a minute it looks like a free-for-all could develop.

Kenny hasn't been the same since the punch in the neck and as his stamina drains away, mine bubbles over. I start prodding him, pushing him almost around the ring. Lining him up and then whacking him. He hasn't taken a terrible battering, but he looks finished. The aura of defeat surrounds him. Like a bullfighter, I sidestep him as he rushes me desperately, and then crash a big left into his face. Kenny sinks to his knees.

'Call it a day, Ken,' shouts a worried voice in the crowd.

'Kill him, Jim,' comes another. But Kenny pushes himself up from the deck with his fists, then complains that he has scraped his knuckles on the concrete. He asks for time to attend to his damaged hands. I nod agreement. Someone steps out the crowd and bathes and cleans his ripped fingers.

Meanwhile, I jump up and down shadow-boxing. With Kenny

Symes, I'm not taking any chances and I don't want to stiffen up. Kenny's not stupid, and it crosses my mind that it could be *him* showboating – maybe he's going to let me think I'm winning and then come in for the kill, taking me by surprise.

I hear someone behind me say that we've been fighting now for 40 minutes. But I'm still feeling good, and when Kenny comes out to resume, I'm all over him like a rash, backing him up until he bends backwards over an old truck. 'Hold it, hold it. Let's get back in the middle,' he snarls.

So I back off him. In the middle again, and I'm landing one solid blow after another. He's going to go over any second. It's like chopping a big old oak down – one blow soon will be the one that topples him.

'Wait, wait.' Kenny bends down and picks up an empty Benson & Hedges packet that is lying on the concrete.

'For fuck's sake, Kenny. If you want to fight, fight. If you don't want to, say so.' This is not Kenny's style – playing for time – but he's a proud man and won't admit when he's beat. He keeps coming and I could knock him out, but hold off. 'Why don't you turn it in, Ken? You're a beaten man today,' I whisper in his ear when we go in close on each other.

'No, I fucking ain't, Stockins.'

So I put three punches into his purr and he just can't reply verbally or physically. 'Come on, big man,' I goad, and then he drops his hands. He's beaten and I've won. Kenny has given best.

But then he gets to rowing with Wally. 'Do you want some, wurzel?' he comes out with, as if it is he who has just finished me off and now it's my brother's turn. Wally replies with a barrage of punches to Kenny's head and he goes down. Knocked clean out.

Then a mush from the crowd steps out and goes fór Wally, so I one-punch him to the ground. The crowd takes on a personality of its own, with people manoeuvring to stand with Kenny's men or ours, others trying to get away. It's going to turn ugly. Someone points to a man and tells Wally he's the one who told him to shut his mouth earlier. The man panics and sets off like a hare, with half the crowd in pursuit. He squeezes through a small gap in the hedge that runs around the perimeter of the site, and the crowd give up the chase. From that day to this, the man has been known as 'Gapinhedge', Gap for short.

Things cool down when Kenny walks over and shakes my hand and we all set off for the Mitcham Mint for our post-fight drinks. The pub is full within seconds and the bar staff can't pull the pints quickly enough. I feel good – I see in the toilet mirror that I'm barely marked. Travellers from all over London are buying me, Wally and Kenny drinks and slapping us on the back.

There was a fair bit of money riding on the fight, because I see fellas pulling out wads of notes and handing them across to others. One man guides me over to a quiet corner and puts a roll of notes into my hand. This was common after a bare-knuckle fight. Both Wally and me have had large amounts of money given to us by happy punters following a fight. Makes you wonder what they have won to feel happy about giving you a £250 or £500 drink.

The celebrations continue all afternoon, and the earlier tension from the site dissolves in a sea of lager, bitter and Guinness. Kenny makes a point of saying to Wally that he's the best man he ever fought. Strange that, seeing that it was me he fought for nigh on an hour. It was Kenny's way of not recognising that I had won. He knew I'd beaten him, but wouldn't accept it. Nevertheless, everyone who was there knows what happened.

I've seen Kenny occasionally since, and there is no bad blood. He is a legend among travellers and fighting folk, one of the all-time great bare-knuckle fighters, who may have been past his best when he challenged me. People mention his name with the greatest respect.

I hear Kenny has found religion and is now a Jehovah's Witness. So, reader, think twice before you slam your front door in the face of a hard-looking man who asks you for a minute of your time.

# 7.

# TOUCHER'S TALE

**TOUCHER HAS BEEN A PAL** most of my life. He's a great fella and a very funny man. When he heard I was doing a book, he said, 'You've got to put my story in, Jim.' I knew what story he meant. There's a fund of Toucher stories because the fella is always up to something, but the one I heard about the night after it happened has become folklore among travellers. Years later, when it turned up in Dave Courtney's book, *Stop the Ride I Want to Get Off*, Toucher was as surprised as anyone. As I said, it happened one night when I wasn't there – so here is Toucher's Tale:

> I've been Jimmy's mate for many years now. Everyone in the gypsy community knows me as Toucher, or Touch for short. Don't ask me why. I got the name as a tiny kid so it's got nothing to do with feeling the ladies up, if that's what you're thinking.
>
> When this bit of a lark happened, I suppose I was about 19. Me and the lads used to meet up on a Saturday night at the Tavern in Langley and then go on to a place called the Queen's Club, which is situated on the Queen's reservoir over near Heathrow Airport. There were a lot of travellers in the vicinity at the time and sometimes we just took this place over.

It was all right for a while, but someone didn't like it and they started getting in bigger and better bouncers. Slowly but surely, they started to stop us coming in, or throwing us out when we were in there. What factory farm they bred these brutes on I don't know. They all looked the same, even though some were black and some were white. Short hair. Fixed grins. Massive chests and shoulders. I couldn't help imagining there was some dwarf behind them who had a tube inserted into their arses and was pounding away on a foot pump.

It wasn't fair though. I don't mean it wasn't fair that we got chucked out, or that we were stopped coming in – that was all part of the game. But these blokes were men, and big fucking men at that, and we were kids. Big kids, I grant you, but it still wasn't fair. Not only that, but the bouncers were nasty. Instead of just dumping you outside on your arse, they'd throw some digs into you and sometimes kick you in the mooey when you were down. They seemed to be practising on us and were enjoying every minute. One idiot even took to using an electric stun gun on us, and roared with laughter, prodding some kid as he was being launched through the doors.

One night I got into a fight in the toilets. Fuck knows what about. Perhaps someone pissed on my dealer boots. Anyway, the bouncers came flying in and picked me up like a piece of copper tubing, one gripping my head, another my feet and two more holding an arm each. They guided me through the dance area like an Exocet missile, and then fired me, cannon-style, out the door.

I picked myself up. 'You liberty-taking cunts!' I shouted at them.

'Go on, get on your donkey and fuck off, you pikey slag,' one replied and all the others laughed, their shoulders heaving up and down like that dog Muttley in the cartoon. Well, I'm Dick Fucking Dastardly and I'm coming back for you boys.

I planned out my revenge. The next night I set out to take

a wheelnut off each wheel of my motor but couldn't find a wheel brace, so I enlisted my two friends from Birmingham, Max and Hickey, to unscrew them.

'Why do you want them off?' enquired Max.

'Because tonight, Max, I'm taking my trusty old catapult out and I'm knocking four coconuts off their shies with it,' I smiled.

Take it from me, I was *the* best shot with a catapult. Everyone knows it. Jimmy's known for being a bare-knuckle man, Joey's a golfer, but me, I'm the man with the sling. I had no choice in the matter really. I can remember being on sites when I was five years of age, lining up bottles of pop and me and the other boys trying to smash them with stones fired from our catapults. I was a natural. It was like a gift. Thank you, God. He gives some people brains, others he makes great athletes or bestows them with money-making skills. Toucher, though, he makes a good catapult man.

It was like the catapult and the missile were an extension of my arm and I could reach out and touch whatever I was aiming at.

But the real reason I became seriously good was that it fell to me to feed the family. My mother walked out one day and never came back, leaving me, Dad and all my little brothers and sisters in the caravan. Dad did his best, but he did take a drink and wasn't around much. Of course, the other travellers helped out, but it wasn't up to them to feed us. They all had big families too.

All these kids crying for food all the fucking time was like having a nest full of baby birds, all with their little beaks open and pointed upward at me. So I took my sling and ventured out into the woods and the farms that surrounded us. Soon, they were the best fed Romany kids in the world, mate. Believe me.

I started bringing home pigeon. They were easy. They are so fucking greedy they get fat and just fall asleep in a tree. You don't even have to creep up. Whack! The first few I shot had exit wounds, I was so close. I soon realised you hardly needed to pull the catapult back to bag these useless bastards. They are the bird equivalent of the fat kid who eats one bag of crisps after another.

Pheasants were a bit harder, but they too are a bit stupid. Early evenings they like to roost low down in the trees, and if you know where they go, you just lie down in the grass and take your time lining one up.

But I started to worry that my brothers and sisters might start growing feathers and cooing, so I started on the rabbits. They don't let you get too close, so your shot has got to be spot on. They normally smell or hear you first at the other end of the field. The old ears go up and start twitching, but before they make the decision to hop off or get back in the warren, you've nigh on taken his head off.

Now and then I'd manage to get a hare. Now they're not easy. Firstly, they are bigger and more agile than the rabbit. You don't see them in groups – distracting each other – and you can't get close in. When they start running, they zig-zag across the field like they know you're trying to shoot them. I respect hares. And jugged hare is bloody lovely and makes it worth the challenge.

Soon, the other travellers got to see and hear about my skill, and when they saw me going out with my sling they'd say, 'Toucher, can you bring us home a partridge, please? And can you fetch a rabbit for old Barney, he's fed up with pigeon.' I was like a Chinese waiter taking orders. I gave all the different birds and animals numbers, so in the end they could ask for a 138 and a 62.

I knew all about balanced diets too, and made sure that I visited the farms and picked apples, pears and cherries. Potatoes, carrots, cabbage, turnips, leeks, onions and parsnips were also not too hard to find, if you knew where to look.

Looking back on it, I should have had a wash, bought a suit and tried to build a supplier relationship with the nearest Sainsburys supermarket.

The next night, I'm back at the Queen's Club. I walked up to the door and five bouncers stepped forward to block my way in. Two of them were different from the previous night, but the others knew who I was. Custer (I'm not sure if we gave him that nickname or he gave it to himself) was there, though, and he was the one I wanted most. He was a bully, not just with us fellas – he made all the young girls give him a kiss before they were allowed in. A nonce case in my book.

'One at a time, you shower of shit,' I said threateningly. The look on their faces said, 'Not this early in the evening, surely,' but they shrugged their shoulders and walked menacingly towards and around me. I stepped backwards. 'Five into one don't go. Come on, one at a time,' I repeated.

I knew they were happy to give me a good hiding, I could see that, so I turned my back on them and walked over to the car to put Plan B into action. 'Shit-outs!' was the last insult I threw over my shoulder before I heard a strange humming noise. Then the metal boomerang hit me on the arm, bounced off and went clean through a car windscreen. So there's me plotting wheelnuts while they were thinking boomerangs.

Still with my back to them, I loaded my catapult with the first heavy old wheelnut and swung around. 'Take cover – he's got a gun,' cried one of the bouncers.

All five of them ran and dived, like Peter Shilton at a penalty shot, behind parked cars. One of them I spotted crouched down behind a car some 25 yards to my right. I got him in my sights and waited. It was just like the old pheasant and me. After several seconds he raised his head to have a look at where I was, just as I knew he would, and I let the nut go. It flew through the evening air like a shooting star and hit this big black bouncer on the jaw. A loud scream pierced the silence and I jelled.

Dave Courtney, in his book, says it was one of the worst things he has ever seen. He writes that the man's jaw nearly dropped to his waist, his tongue rolled out like a carpet and his teeth sprayed across the floor like broken mints. I wasn't hanging around to have a look though. I jumped in the motor and sped off, although I heard a few bottles and glasses land on the roof. I was pleased with a job well done.

A couple of days later, the gavvers paid me a visit. 'Have you had any trouble down at the Queen's lately, Toucher?' they asked.

'No, sir, I never goes there these days.' He's in plain clothes with a bunch of uniforms crowded into my trailer behind him. In most trailers, there's a shelf on the right-hand side of the door as you go in. I dump my money and change on there, and anything else from my pockets. I glance over and see my catapult with the sling neatly tied around sitting there. The plain-clothes man is almost brushing it with his hand. 'Someone nearly got killed there the other night,' continued the Old Bill man.

'That's why I don't go there no more.'

I had my defence ready in case they did have something on me. I was going to say he threw a metal boomerang at me and it came back and took his jaw off. Might have worked.

All of them carried on looking around the trailer without actually moving anything. They obviously didn't have a warrant. Whether or not they were looking for a catapult I don't know, but they never saw the thing stuck right under their noses. They left and I heard no more about it. I did hear that the bouncer was okay after a while and that he packed up the licensed bullying game. Just goes to show that whoever you are, no matter how big you are, how many weights you can lift, how nice you look in your black suit and little dicky-bow, there's always someone who'll wipe the smirk off your face.

My fame as a hotshot with a catapult spread all over. Once I was asked to demonstrate my skills to a group of travellers. They picked one of their number and got him to stand some 20 yards away with a can of Budweiser on his head. 'Knock that off,' they dared.

I was happy to oblige. I'd had about ten cans of Bud myself and was up for anything, but I'm not sure that the mush with the can on his head was too happy about it. He was only about 16. I trained my eye on the tin and thankfully the pebble I used sailed through space and took it clean off his head. It landed some way behind him. Then they asked me to do it again but I thought better of it. The boy visibly relaxed, as the gypsy William Tell put his catapult away.

Toucher's recipe for a good ole traditional Romany meal:

| | | |
|---|---|---|
| STARTER | Hedgehogs | Bake in clay, remove spikes and cut meat into succulent small slices. Serve with tandoori sauce. |
| MAIN COURSE | Joey Grey | Slice potatoes, mushrooms, tomatoes, bacon/rabbit/chicken, add 2 Oxo cubes and water. Cook as stew. |
| *or* | Bacon Pudding | Shape meat suet into a pudding a foot long. Inside lay bacon, onions and tomatoes. Wrap in cloth and boil for 2 hours. |
| VEGETARIAN OPTION | Sheep Partge | Take a sheep's gut and clean the lining. Cut into small squares and boil for 3–4 hours. Serve with vegetables and crusty bread. Very sweet. |
| DESSERT | | Coffee and After Eight mints. |

I had a fight about the same time as Toucher's escapade, with a Slough man who had a big reputation. He was a gorger with a bit of traveller in him, I think, but locally they was all scared of the fella. I knew of him and kept out of his way.

One day, I had been drinking since lunchtime with Boo Gardner and his brother Ferg. We fancied some smoke to take the edge off the drink, so we headed through Colnbrook to a house where we could normally score a bit of puff. Maybe we were too drunk, or they didn't have any gear, but they didn't answer the door although we knew these dealers were inside. Don't know why I did it, but when we gave up knocking, I slung a brick through the window.

Halfway down the road, a car flashes past us and cuts us up, making us stop. Billy, the Slough face, jumps out and three or four geezers are behind him. 'What did you do that for?' he demands.

Now Billy, by all accounts, can have a row. His mates look up for it too. Boo Gardner and his brother are not fighting men, and they shouldn't have to be on my account, so I didn't show any aggression towards Billy. 'I don't know,' I replied, with some honesty.

He hits me with two shots and I slump back against the car. I am well pissed, but I know it is better to live to fight another day. He's draped over me, asking if I want more. 'No, mate, no,' I say. He gives me another slap and then triumphantly swaggers back to his motor. Jimmy Stockins is obviously not the man he heard I was. The man with the big reputation has added that gypo streetfighter's scalp to his belt, or so he thought.

Next day, I went round to Wally's and told him all about it. 'I'm going round there now to fight the man,' I told Wally, who came along to see fair play. I knew where he lived, roughly, found the house and went up and banged on his door. The last thing he expected was me knocking on his front door at nine o'clock in the morning. The milkman, yes – the gypsy, no.

He came out into his garden with a massive Rottweiler foaming at the mouth and straining on its chain. Billy, not the dog, started growling at me.

'Billy, put the dog away. Me and you are going to take a walk to that little field over there and we're going to have ourselves a fight.'

He still didn't speak, just kept growling and moving his head around like a demented chicken as I stood there calmly. Finally, he shoved the dog in the kitchen door and came back out, jumping up and down and thrusting his head forward. If I didn't know better, it could have been some strange mating ritual they do over in Slough.

By now, a handful of neighbours had come out their houses and followed us into the field. 'I'm like a mad dog,' he warned me. 'I'm gonna rip your fucking head off.' To be absolutely honest, for all his mouth, he was one of the most useless men I ever fought. His punches didn't really land and they had no snap. Once I hit him, he folded up. He gave up before I could knock the man out, which disappointed me. So I humiliated him a bit in front of his neighbours and then agreed to shake his hand. Maybe he was good in the pub, with all his dramatics and the glasses and ashtrays flying around, but in an empty field with the dew still on the grass he was a fairy.

That chavvy brings to mind another nutter I got tangled up with in more recent times. I was with Cousin Joe and a couple of other friends in the Green Man in Wraysbury. There was a group of young men drinking in there and playing pool. They were not typical Chelsea supporter types; more like students. But one of them, who I later learned was the son of a local doctor, didn't like gypsies for some reason. We could hear him spitting out insults: fucking gypos this, dirty pikeys that. Benny was his name.

Finally, I said something to him and he got the fight he was spoiling for. I easily beat the man, but he kept coming back and getting up every time I floored him. He either had a lot of courage or he was just plain daft. I finally launched him out the door and we thought that was the end of it, but within a few minutes he was back charging at us again. This time I went to town on him, and again he fought and fought and fought. Finally I kicked him out the door, thoroughly bruised and battered.

We didn't expect him back, but a few minutes later the door opened again and we heard him scream, 'Gypsy cunts!' He was covered in blood and we knew the only way to shut this man up was to put him down for good. Not wishing to kill a man for having a lot of bottle, we finished our drinks and headed off.

Working on this book, I tried to cast my mind back to the first bare-knuckle fight I ever witnessed and I can remember it now. It was back on that disused airfield in Hornchurch, when I was about seven years old. The airfield was huge and we all came out to look curiously when about 150 Irish travellers pulled on. They gathered over on the other side of the field from us and kept themselves to themselves, but us kids couldn't resist wandering over and taking a look. At the time, we hadn't really come across the Irish in big numbers. Their language was different and they seemed very boisterous, shouting and arguing with one another.

Within half an hour of their arrival, two of the men were stripped to the waist and fighting one another. While we watched with our mouths wide open, the womenfolk continued to busy themselves setting up their trailers and most of the other men were humping around generators and water containers as if nothing was going on.

After a while, one Irishman, smothered in blood, had had enough and his friend stepped in to take his place. Then, half an hour later, the first man touched someone else's hand and a new man took his place – bare-knuckle tag fighting if you will.

This went on for hours. They only stopped when dusk fell and they decided it was time to go off to the pub. We heard them come back that night all singing and shouting, but the next afternoon they started the fighting again.

On the second evening, one enormous man came over to our fire to borrow something. His shirt was off and as I stared at the flat expanse of his bare back, I saw a mosaic of scars and stab wounds. I knew all about fighting by then. It was in my family. But all the fighters I knew fought for sport, honour or from fury – these were the first people I had ever come across who fought purely for fun.

## 8.

# THE GAVVERS

FROM AN EARLY AGE gypsy kids are always watching what goes on around them. It's in the blood, I suppose. As a traveller you live off your wits and learn how to look after yourself. You have to know who to trust and who not to. With gorgers, we start off by assuming they are all out to do us down in some way, unless proved otherwise. I guess gorgers feel the same way about gypsies. The times I've heard people say, 'I was drinking with the gypos last night. They're not too bad really. Got the drinks in . . .' Some people seem genuinely surprised when we don't beat them up, steal their money, flick ash on their carpets and when we actually flush their toilet after using it.

When the photographer came on our site to take some pictures for this book, I could see he was terrified. I put my arm around him and said, 'Don't worry, mate, we ain't going to eat you . . . yet,' and we all laughed. At the end, he thanked me. For what? Not choring his equipment? Not infecting him with a disease?

But the people we learn to distrust, with no ifs and buts, are the gavvers, the Old Bill, the garlos, the police. My earliest memories of them are when we'd pull onto a bit of land and they would come along with the farmer to persuade us to move on. Then they'd be back, escorting some geezer in a suit from the courts or the council, serving an eviction notice. We could see our parents were cross and harassed and we immediately saw the police as the people who were trying to stop us living our traditional lives.

However, unlike the farmer or the fella from the council, the police often seemed to take a pleasure in pushing us around. We were vermin who caused trouble wherever we went, and it was up to them to extinguish us. Soon as we got anywhere, they'd be over: a lady had complained that the smoke from our bonfire had dirtied her washing; there had been a spate of stolen milk from doorsteps; newspapers had been taken out of letterboxes (like we read a lot of papers), and all the usual old shit that is levelled at us wherever we stop. Try ringing the police about your next-door neighbour's bonfire and see how quickly they come around to deal with that.

Of course, it is in our blood to be wary of the police and the law. Remember, we are about the only people on earth born criminal. The very nature of our nomadic lifestyle puts us on the wrong side of the law. It wasn't too long ago that it was a criminal offence in this country merely to be a gypsy. Only 250 years ago men and women were being hung up and down the country for this terrible offence. Some say that in the Middle Ages, the Church, who ran the show in those days, triggered the anti-gypsy movement because they saw them as a threat. They didn't want the common people finding enlightenment having their palms read and not going to church.

I first got loud when I was 15. Two pals, Lesley and Tommy Boswell, and me was driving an old Ford Anglia, when we ran out of petrol. The car wasn't stolen or anything like that, but technically we were too young to be on the road. 'I don't believe it,' said my pal, who was driving, 'we're clean out of juice. We either nick some or we're walking home.'

We found a parked car, stuffed a length of tubing into the tank and siphoned out a gallon of petrol. As we walked back to our motor with the can, the gavvers cruised past and we chucked the can in the air and bolted. I tripped and fell, and was captured. I ended up in court for the first time and received a conditional discharge.

The next time I got nicked was over a roofing job in Romford. I charged £80 for the work, but the customers complained to the police because I had told them it would cost £40. When I had said it would cost £40, that's what I thought at the time. There was more to it once I got working. This time I was charged with deception and received a small fine.

After my Dad dying, when I took to heavy drinking, it was on the cards that I'd be crossing paths with the gavvers more often. Also, through my fighting I now had a bit of a reputation, and they seemed to be more aware of me and who I was.

We were in the White Hart pub in Mitcham, the one which overlooks the cricket green, when I was nicked for something that resulted in my first experience of prison. We used this pub often and sometimes got a bit boisterous, but on the whole there was no real trouble. The guvnor served us afters, and seemed to like having us around. Mitcham can be a very rough place and he looked upon us as unpaid protection, I think. As is often the case with these things, nothing was said or written, but we'd keep ourselves just about under control and were quick to stop any fights between others. We also stopped some of the people he wasn't keen on coming in. In return, sometimes he'd give us a round on the house. One evening I walked in early, sober as a judge, and was wrestled to the ground by about ten burly gavvers. They threw me into the back of a waiting car and said I was under arrest for threatening to kill the landlord. Then they drove in a convoy, lights flashing and sirens blaring, to the station, which was all of 100 yards away. What a performance!

I was remanded in Brixton prison for three days until me and Nicky Deighton, who was apparently planning to kill the landlord with me, were given bail. Neither of us ever threatened to kill that landlord, not even in jest. I think he had decided he wanted us out and maybe that we'd taken over his pub a bit too much. I suppose he thought we might threaten to kill him if he said that he no longer wanted us around, but that's a different matter. Or maybe it was the police that persuaded him to trump up some allegations against me.

Whatever, the landlord, his wife and their staff put on the performance of a lifetime when the trial finally came around. They were painting me and Nicky as gangsters who demanded lager and lime with menaces, but there was no substance to it. Despite that, we got a guilty verdict and I copped 12 months. Poor old Nicky was given 18 months.

I began my sentence in Wormwood Scrubs and from there I was shipped out to Camp Hill prison on the Isle of Wight. Camp Hill was one hard prison, with a potential murderer waiting around every corner. When they get fed up with you in other jails, they send you over there.

Brother Wally had the misfortune of sampling all three prisons on the island: Parkhurst, Albany and Camp Hill, and says that compared to Camp Hill the other two were like the Ritz Hotel. I'm not sure how many times Wally has stayed at the Ritz, but that is what he says.

I hated it. Prison is bad enough for anyone, but for travellers it is a form of torture. We are used to fresh air and moving around, eating when we want, shitting where and when we want and not being told what to do by anyone. Everything we are bred to avoid is in the nick. I really did feel like a cock linnet in a cage. If a traveller kept his lurcher dog locked up in the toilet for 23 hours a day, there'd be hell to pay. Now I know the lurcher hasn't threatened to kill a publican (allegedly), but nevertheless it was a harsh punishment. And one thing's for sure – you ain't going to reform no man by keeping him in a cell for 23 hours out of every 24.

I still do not know what the rationale behind the prison system is. Is it to reform? Is it to punish? Is it to protect? Maybe it's a bit of all three. Maybe it is one of those for some, and another for others. Whatever it is, there is no consistency.

I have no problem with accepting punishment when you have done wrong and you get caught. That is the risk you take. I can even live with getting a guilty verdict for something you are not guilty of if you've got away with lots in the past. But what is all wrong is the inconsistencies in the sentences and time served.

If, for example, society demands that all murderers serve life, that's fine by me. If they dictate that all murderers should only serve six years, then I will have to live with that. But you shouldn't be able to have it both ways. The late Reg Kray, serving 31 years for murder whilst others serve less than five is an extreme case, but the system is full of these anomalies.

Everyone else in prison seemed to pass the time by reading books, and for the first time in my life I wished I could read, if only to take my mind off doing the bird. I couldn't read letters either, or send any out for that matter, but there was always someone who would do it for you. Truth was, though, I wasn't going to get much in the way of letters from my family and friends, most of them being in the same boat as me as far as reading and writing goes.

In a way I was glad, because I could see how much the men depended on their letters. They'd read them over and over. Analyse every word. Ask their cellmates what they thought. Sometimes they'd get all paranoid about them, reading between the lines, literally. Their moods for the following days could sometimes depend on their last letter, or the letter that didn't come.

I decided to keep my head down and my nose clean. The place was full of headbangers, and all I needed was for it to get around that there was a gypsy bare-knuckle fighter on the block with an attitude problem. Luckily, no one bothered me and I didn't bother anyone. Even the screws treated me well.

I was also lucky enough to find that a fella from Mitcham, by the name of Steve Lowe, was also on the island. Lowey had some traveller in him and was a good man. He made me laugh, and made the sentence easier to serve.

After eight months I was released, and couldn't get off the island quick enough. As the ferry chugged away back to Portsmouth, I looked back at the shoreline and wondered what the Isle of Wight was actually like. I'd lived there for eight months and hadn't seen any of it. It seemed strange. People go there for holidays, so it must have something besides prisons, screws and their families.

---

I returned to the site in Epsom and settled back into a routine. I'd done some weight training in prison and was the fittest I'd been for a while, so I got back to running and keeping myself in trim. I used the pubs in Epsom mainly, and got in the habit of having a pint in each one as I walked from the site to the town centre. I'd take in the King's Arms, the Locomotive, the Plough and Harrow, the Rifleman and the Spread Eagle. Then I'd wander over to the Clock Tower, where they held the market, and have a hot-dog or a hamburger before meandering back home.

The hot-dog stall was a focal point for young people after the pubs had closed in Epsom. Youths from the pubs and courting couples in cars would converge on it at weekends, and people would sit around on their bonnets drinking coffee and chewing burgers. Jacked-up or alloy wheels and musical horns stick in my mind. The boys all opened their car doors so the music blared out and competed. Sometimes fights broke out between the lads, and now and then bikers turned up and there would be free-for-alls. These were not my fights, and I kept out of them all. But it could be a pretty lawless place. One time, the burger man told me, the Epsom boys took on the whole Epsom Old Bill and gave them a hiding, and a dozen or so of them ended up at the Old Bailey for their pains.

I got friendly with the hamburger man and he looked after me with cups of tea and burgers, so I started to look after him. If people got lairy with him or refused to pay, I'd have a word and normally they'd ease off. If the boys wanted to fight I'd make sure they were not too near the stall. I should have known better after the White Hart fiasco, but a relationship developed. I would unofficially mind him and the stall at the weekends from the rowdy elements. Occasionally, he'd give me a tenner and sometimes I asked for one. My burgers and tea were always gratis.

One night, after Lowey had come out, we were sitting in the stall after a night's drinking. Lowey rolled a joint and the man started cooking us a burger each. 'Windy tonight, Jim,' says the burger man.

'Yeah, a bit,' I says, tugging on Lowey's spliff.

'Be no good tonight, Jim,' he went on, 'no customers means no money. Eh, Jim?'

'Don't worry, mate. It'll pick up later, when the wine bar throws out and the Welly and the Spread shut up.'

Lowey looks at me and lifts an eyebrow. The spliff nearly gets us giggling, over what I'm not sure.

'It's raining now, Jim. There won't be no money tonight, for you or for me.' I wasn't listening. He did mumble on at times.

Some friends arrived. 'Sort them out with some burgers,' I said and our man obliged.

After an hour or so, Lowey and me decided to head home, so we got up and, in front of the stall-owner, I took a few pound notes from the till. But as we stepped down from the wagon, the Old Bill pounced, put me and Lowey's hands up our backs and cuffed us. Then we were thrown into a police van and taken back to Epsom nick.

At the police station, I couldn't believe the furore. There were vans and police everywhere, sirens wailing and dogs barking. Anyone would think they had captured Carlos the Jackal and Ronnie Biggs having an Indian meal together in Epsom High Street.

Perhaps they thought a gang of armed gypsies would storm the police station – that's not as fanciful as it seems, because back in the First World War, the gavvers here in Epsom arrested a Canadian soldier following an altercation in the Rifleman pub, and his fellow soldiers, who were stationed in the area, stormed the station and freed the man. A local policeman was killed, and there is a plaque on the wall commemorating the incident.

Standing in front of the sergeant, he read us the charges solemnly. We were all ears. Demanding money with menaces.

We were remanded in custody, then it was back to the Scrubs and on to Brixton. A week turned into a month, and before I knew it we'd been on remand for six months. After nearly a year in prison, unconvicted, the case reached the Old Bailey.

Again, it seemed over the top: taking the piss out of the burger man and nicking a bit of money from him. Is that really what the Old Bailey is for? Mind you, after the way my old man's case went, nothing surprised me about the justice system any more.

Lowey was acquitted halfway through, but they persisted with me. They played a tape from that night which explained the man's odd attempts at conversation with me. The police had obviously wired him up. If anything, I think the tape went in my favour. There was no demanding money with menaces on it. Even the burgers for our friends were asked for ever so nicely. All you could really hear was me and Lowey sucking in draw. But there was no getting away from the fact that I had taken money from the till. The notes had all been marked, because the police were the ones that put them in there in the first place.

At the end of the trial, the jury could not reach a verdict. The judge ordered a retrial, and this time I was released on bail.

A new trial commenced nine months later at the Old Bailey and we went through the whole stupid thing again. This time, I was found not guilty. I was well pleased that the case which had been hanging over me for nearly two years was finally over and a sensible verdict had been reached.

I was wrong to take money from that man, but I shouldn't have served a year inside for it. Not once did he ask me to leave the stall or complain in any way, and it wasn't because he was scared. I had never threatened him. He had asked me to help him with troublesome people a number of times and he didn't deny that. I provided him with a service and he paid me for it. But I should have known better and so should he. What with the fight at the wedding, mentioned earlier, and now this, I was beginning to wonder if there was a jinx over me and cheeseburgers.

Brother Wally, despite his promising pro boxing career, also got himself in plenty of trouble after Dad died and, like me, found himself doing the bird a number of times in his twenties. One time, he was serving a four-and-a-half-year sentence in Highpoint, which the cons jokingly called Knifepoint. It wasn't very funny, though, because Highpoint was a C category jail with a history of trouble. Stabbings were a regular event, hence the nickname. Wally takes up the story:

I had been in Knifepoint nearly six months when a good friend and travelling boy called Mark Kupper comes into the jail. He and I kept each other company and we started sparring and keeping fit. Then we were joined by two other travellers, both known to me: Frank Jones and Hallner, so we had a right little band of gypsies in the nick.

Frank soon gets to work dealing tobacco, smoke and phone cards – the stock prison currencies. Another man seems to be running the nick, and first of all him and Frank deal together.

This other man is meant to be an ex-serviceman who has served with the Royal Marines as a commando, but he likes his drugs and has somehow ended up in here. He certainly looks the part, marching around the prison with his chest out and back straight, as if he's on parade. Most of the cons, and even some of the screws, give him a wide berth because he's rumoured to be a bit of a bully and tasty with his fists. Soon, him and Frank fall out over some money or baccy that is owed: Frank says he's a greedy bastard and he ain't going to pay him what he owes.

One afternoon, Frank and me are walking along a footpath between billets where all the cons are housed when the ex-soldier barges up to Frank and sneers into his face. 'Pay up time!'

Frank pushes him away and he shoves Frank back, so I stand in between them and tell them to break it up. Fighting in prison means you both lose, every time. 'Fuck off, you little no-good pikey,' the commando spits. 'I've never liked you,' and he looks down into my eyes, trying to scare me. Frank's argument has become my fight. 'All right, mush, let's go behind the huts and sort it out.' And that's what we do.

By the time me and action man are shaping up, about 50 cons have sussed on and nipped behind the huts, a blind spot as far as the screws in the yard were concerned. I'd been there before. I liked this – crowds of men gathering around to watch me fight. It lifted my spirits and made me feel nostalgic for the days fighting outside on the rolling hills of Epsom Downs, or between the trailers on a safe site.

My first punch, which I drill into his jaw, puts him down but he quickly gets up. He knows I can punch now so he keeps his hands high, but this exposes his rib cage and I catch him, one, two, bang-bang to the body. He drops down to protect his torso, so I just do his jaw again. Down he goes and then gets up once more. But I won't leave his jaw alone and he goes straight back down. This time he mumbles, through a mouth full of blood, that he's had enough.

What I didn't know at the time was that two screws were watching the whole thing from the window of a cell where they were carrying out a search. An alarm bell was sounded and the commando and me were led off to the punishment block. The next morning, after a night banged up in solitary, we were up in front of the governor. As governors go, she was all right.

We are stood in front of her between two big screws, with two others standing behind us for good measure. Two more screws are brought in, the ones who witnessed the fight, and they begin to give evidence against us. She ain't no fool and looks at them sternly. 'Did you two men see this fight from the beginning?' she interrupts their flow.

'Yes, ma'am.'

'Then why did it take you more than five minutes to sound the alarm?'

The screws couldn't answer.

'Good fight, was it?'

'Yes, ma'am,' the screws eventually reply, shamefaced.

'And who won?' she continues, fixing her eyes on us.

'Wally did, ma'am,' volunteers the commando. 'He beat me fair and square.' Fair and square or not, we both lose seven days' remission, but the spat gave me some respect in the prison. After it, other inmates even came to me to mediate in rows.

After 14 months with no further blots on my copybook, they shipped me out to Ford open prison in West Sussex to finish my sentence and live the comparatively luxurious life of a D-cat. Ford is a funny old place. Besides people like me, nearing the end of their sentences, it caters for people who couldn't cope with 'real' prison: people like bent coppers, mortgage fraudsters, drunk drivers and so on. The footballer George Best and Ernest Saunders of Guinness scandal fame both spent a bit of time in here.

I'd been here before. Last time, I was in with my brother-in-law Tom, and to pass the time of the day we'd work out in the gym. Banging away on the old punch bag one day was a fella named Tommy Carson, who they reckon once felt Ken Buchanan. Remember him – the Scottish boxer with the tartan shorts who went on to become a world champion? Tommy had a rep in prison, because of being connected with some of the big criminal families.

On seeing me, he threw over a pair of gloves. 'I hear you can box, boy,' he smiled. I assumed he just wanted a spar and thought nothing about slipping the gloves on and shaping up, but he came straight into me and started punching my fucking head in. 'Hold up!' I shouted, as I tried to protect my head with my arms.

He is out of order, because if you're caught with a mark on your face here they know you've been fighting, and you're shipped straight back to a C-cat jail. It is irrelevant who started the row.

Tommy grinned and came at me again as I walked backwards around the gym. I slipped his next punch and caught him with a left-right combo to the face. Then I give him a dozen body shots and he dropped to his knees complaining about the pain in his sides. I slipped the gloves off and fucked

off out before anyone came. He can take the flak. He started it – I just finished it. Turned out he suffered a broken jaw and two cracked ribs.

Not much happens in prison, so our fight was the talk of the place for a while. Ambrose Mendy, Nigel Benn's former manager, was in at the time and he invited me to his room for tea. There were pictures of boxers all over the walls and he really played up the whole celebrity thing. He said he'd heard I'm a good boxer, and that he thought I had a lot of potential. To be honest, I didn't take him very seriously. I never saw anything more of Tommy Carson, and as for Ambrose Mendy, the last I heard, he was caught in the safety net between the landings of a nick after being chucked over the railings following a row over phone cards.

One incident, which happens a lot, took place in one of the prisons I was in, although the authorities wouldn't admit it. It was a D-cat jail – I won't say which one, because there is no point getting anyone in trouble, not even a screw. A huge black man arrived on the wing. He was six-feet-something with a shaved bonce, but for all his hard-man looks, he kept himself to himself. Me, Brian Green and Danny Penfold had a little team together at the time and one afternoon a screw we had a reasonable relationship with called me to one side. 'Wally, I wonder if you'd like to do me a small favour? You know the new black fella? Well, he shouldn't be on this wing. Do you get my drift?'

'Why not?'

'He's a nonce, Wally. He raped a 14-year-old girl. He should be on Rule 43 with the others. I don't know why they've put him in here. I've got children, Wally, as I'm sure you have.'

We didn't need much persuading. The officer explained we had one minute to attack him before they would intervene. I told the others, and as the rapist walked past my cell I jumped out and chinned him with all my might. Down he went. One of the others set about him with that favourite prison weapon, a tin of Heinz baked beans in a sock. Within seconds, the floor area around his head was awash with a smelly mixture of blood and the slightly less red-coloured baked bean sauce. No charges were laid, and the sex case was put on Rule 43.

You meet some real cranks in prison. When I was in a cell with my brother-in-law Tom, they brought a third man into share with us. He was one of these body-building types. There are a lot of them in the prison system. Many of them are men of previous good character, so I reckon all these steroids they take send them mad. This bloke used to lie on his bed reading a body-building magazine all the time, and when he wanted to get off his bunk he would roll off and land on his outstretched arms.

I don't know whether we were meant to be impressed by that, but he wasn't too happy when I said to Tom, 'Eh, bruv, I think they've put a woofter in here with us.' Charles Atlas didn't take too kindly to that and demanded I spar with him there and then. The geezer was musclebound. I shot a couple up his ribs before he could draw back his fist and he lay there moaning. He didn't grass, but next day he got himself moved to another cell.

Towards the end of a later sentence, they move me and a bunch of other prisoners from Wormwood Scrubs to Camp Hill on the Isle of Wight to finish our sentences. Imagine my surprise when we stop off on the route and my brother Wally is led on to the coach! They attach him to the chain that runs the length of the aisle and we sit next to each other. Wally is off to Albany to serve his sentence, and this time he's copped a six-and-a-half slap.

There are no dirty videos or refreshments on HMP Luxury Coaches, so we just talk. We're so pleased and surprised to see each other that we can't stop chattering with excitement.

On the boat from Portsmouth we are still all chained together, so

God knows what would happen should the boat go down or the bloke next to you start chucking up with seasickness. With our noses pressed up against the window, looking out at the Solent, Wally says quietly: 'Just think, bruv, in a couple of months you'll be sailing back across the water on your way home.' A big lump comes to my throat, because Wally is looking at four years at least before he gets out. I want to embrace him but can't. I even consider doing something stupid, like gouging a screw's eyes with my thumbs, so I can get more bird and stay with my brother, but I know that the last thing they would do is put us together.

Wally had a torrid time in Albany. He met up with a couple of familiar faces in there, Pat McCann for one, but on only his second day he ended up in a fight. Wally had wandered into the TV room and as no one seemed to be paying any attention to what was on, he got up and changed the channel. Horse racing was on, and that suited Wally fine. Like I said, though, little things in prison can suddenly get blown out of all proportion and a big mush, who Wally hadn't even noticed, jumped up and turned the channel back. 'Anyone who touches that telly again has me to deal with,' he growled. Wally duly turned it straight back.

'Right, you,' ordered the bloke, who Wally found out later was a lifer whose day consisted of doing weights and watching telly, 'down the corridor, now!' He was pointing in that direction and wanted Wally to follow him there. But Wally, whose strength was always his fantastic speed, planted six or seven punches on him literally before he knew what had hit him. The lifer went down and then the two of them were overpowered by a bunch of screws who marched them down to the block.

Wally's ruck was nothing compared to what was about to happen. By all accounts, the prison was out of control, with the cons openly walking about and administering beatings and cutting each other up whilst the screws turned a blind eye. Within a few months of Wally being there, the prison went up and there was a full-scale riot. Prisoners got on the roof, and for a day or two the prison was under the control of the cons. I heard about all this on the radio, but soon our screws took away our radios, TVs and newspapers in case we got ideas. Then they banged us up for 24 hours a day whilst they nipped next door to help quell the riots.

I wondered where Wally fitted in. I couldn't imagine him just sitting there in his cell until it died down. He told me afterwards, though, that he did exactly that. Seeing first prisoners, and then screws, being dragged past his cell leaving trails of blood freaked him out, and he decided to keep his head down.

It turned out that the IRA prisoners in Albany wanted to serve the remainder of their sentences in Ireland and be allowed to wear their own clothes instead of prison uniform. Then the Mufti squad came in, and over five days regained control of the jail. Wally said they were ruthless bastards, dressed in black boilersuits and crash helmets with visors, carrying riot shields and long batons. He told me he saw some merciless hidings and was amazed no one died.

Every now and then, Wally said, a piece of rope would dangle outside his cell window. Any food you had was to be tied to the string so the Irishmen could pull it up on to the roof and last a bit longer. However, if the screws caught you helping the IRA protestors, you could expect 90 days' lost remission.

Besides the paddies, Albany was full of high-profile prisoners. The mastermind behind the Knightsbridge safe deposit robbery was in there, as was one of the Iranians from the Iranian Embassy siege as well as the alleged murderers of the paper boy, Carl Bridgewater. Later, these men staged their own rooftop protests. Wally had been in another jail with one of the Hickey brothers, and was convinced that no way did they kill the boy. Years later, a court of appeal agreed and they were freed, but by then they had served many, many years.

Finally, after the jail was calmed following the riot, the governor called for Wally and told him that he and 19 others had the job of rebuilding the jail, redecorating it and cleaning it up. Everyone else had been shipped out except for them, and the governor promised that if they did a good job he'd make sure they got a C-cat or D-cat jail and would do whatever else he could for them.

It was all kept quiet – the governor didn't want to admit that the IRA had basically shut his prison down. Eighteen months it took, from clearing up the debris to laying slabs, from washing down walls to repainting. It was backbreaking work, but the men were treated well and were allowed to cook their own meals from the microwave (mainly because the kitchens had been destroyed in the riots).

The governor was true to his word and, when the job was finished, he arranged for Wally to finish his sentence in Northeye prison, down near Hastings in Sussex. After just a few months tidying the gardens and working in the stores he was called before the governor. 'I've got some good news and some bad news for you, Wally,' he said.

'Give me the bad news first,' Wally said, preparing for another blow.

'The bad news is you are getting no more home leave.'

'But why, sir?'

'Because, Wally, you are going home.'

## 9.

# FROM EDMONTON WITH LOVE

**FOLLOWING MY EVENTUAL ACQUITTAL** of the Great Epsom Burger Protection Racket, I decided it was time to move on before the police set me up for stealing pear drops from Woolworth's or assaulting someone with a clump of heather.

By this time, I was with my wife Lydia and she was pregnant with our first baby. We met in a Woolwich pub and I got talking to her at the bar. She was just 16 and very pretty. Her Dad was none too keen on us getting together, but that wasn't going to stop us. Like Mum and Dad before us, we eloped and returned a couple. First of all we stayed over at West Drayton and then settled for a bit at Waltham Cross, where our daughter Charmaine was born.

At last, I felt like I was straightening out and my private rage and grief was subsiding. I was with a woman I loved and now I had a child. Life was getting better.

Wally was doing fine too, enjoying life. He was always a live wire. Always up to something. Like Dad, he enjoyed a bet, and I remember one time when he went to the dog racing at White City. He was with cousin Jack. They were both flush after having completed a building job, and had £500 each on them. They told each other, knowing what they were both like, that they must hold back £10 each to ensure they could get a cab back to Epsom should they do their bollocks. Of course, they did do their bollocks, and their last tenners went on a bet to get them out of the shit. But these last two punts predictably failed and they were left penniless.

Full of drink, they set off on the long walk from Shepherd's Bush to Epsom. By the time they hit the Fulham Palace Road, their enthusiasm for a hike had worn off like the drink, and Wally spotted two pushbikes leant up against the side wall of a house. They chored them and pedalled off furiously in the direction of Putney Bridge. Wally says one of the funniest moments of his life was looking over his shoulder on the A3 road to see cousin Jack pedalling like a madman behind him. Jack had got the short straw – a tiny kid's bike, and he was shouting at Wally to slow down, as his adult legs practically hit his chin each time the wheels went round. Unbelievably, they got home without a pull from the police and the bikes were donated to a charity for underprivileged gypsy children.

Wally had some trouble around this time with a man from a site over in Banstead. They called him Tyson, after the young boxer who was just breaking through. Or *he* called himself Tyson, anyway. Wally was visiting a dying relative of his wife's at St George's Hospital in Tooting, when from behind those rubbery swing-doors you get in hospitals a fist appeared and whacked him several times. Before Wally could recover, the attacker was gone.

Not wanting to cause too much of a scene with his wife's family at this time, he nevertheless asked who had done it. No one would say.

'Okay, if you don't tell me I'm going to come to where each one of you stays and fight you one by one until you tell me.' Finally, an old boy among them told Wally who it was – Tyson. Wally knew him by name and by sight, but had no idea why the mush should want to dell him and then jell.

He went back to the Lonesome site in Streatham, which was close by, to freshen up, and then drove over to Banstead where he knew Tyson was staying. Problem was, Wally didn't know which trailer was his and no one on there would tell him, so he walked around the site shouting for him to come outside and fight. Like the little Chinese man in the Peter Sellers *Pink Panther* films, Tyson did appear, jumping off a six-foot-high fence onto Wally's back. It certainly surprised my brother, because the bloke got a good ten punches in on his face before Wally could shake him off. Wally was fuming by now, because Tyson had on some big gold sovereign rings and they had gouged his cheeks a bit.

'I'll fight you in the morning for £200,' challenged Tyson as Wally advanced on him.

'No, let's do it now.'

'All right, £400 in the morning,' blurted out Tyson, playing for time as he sensed that Wally wanted to kill him.

A wager of £400 swayed even an angry Wally. 'You're on,' he said.

'If you don't turn up and start the fight at ten on the dot, then you owe me £400 without a punch being thrown. Agreed?' asked Tyson.

Wally agreed, but he couldn't see what the man was getting at. He phoned me and told me all about it. I knew of Tyson too, and suspected he hit Wally in the hospital just to make a name for himself, but the arrangements sounded like a bit of a set up to me. I told Wally I'd be there in the morning and that I was bringing a few of the boys just in case.

'Don't forget to be there at ten exactly, Jim,' Wally reminded me as he put the phone down.

My brother arrived on the site at ten to ten and Tyson was ready, along with a good 100 people gathered. 'I'm waiting for my brother first,' explained Wally, 'just to see fair play.'

By ten, though, I still hadn't got there. I was close, but the traffic was heavy. Tyson said, 'Sorry, Wally, it's dead on ten. You owe me £400.'

Wally cracked him hard up the rib cage and Tyson vomited. Green-coloured sick oozed from his mouth and trickled down his chin. Wally moved in and put one on his jaw and Tyson sunk to his knees. 'I've had enough,' he gasped. Two-punch Tyson. Seems that he was more like Cicely Tyson than Mike Tyson.

I pulled in and jumped out the car. As far as I was concerned, I was more or less on time. Billy, Tommy and Charlie Brown were with me. 'Anyone want to fight?' I asked, scouring the hundred or so faces looking at us. We're well outnumbered, but I figured the best form of defence is attack. Then I turned to Tyson, who was looking at me. 'Do you want to fight me instead?' I demanded.

'No, it's all right, Jim, I've just done him,' Wally informed me.

'You want to change your name from Tyson, I think,' I told the man, falling in now with what's happened. 'Go and get your money to pay my brother.'

Tyson sloped off to beg and borrow the cash to pay Wally when one man in the crowd stepped forward and said, 'I'll fight you.' It was Tyson's brother-in-law. He had some bottle, but was really just going through the motions. I hit him with some feeler shots to the head and then a few more to the body. The man dropped his hands and gave best before he even hit me back. A strange little ending to a strange little episode.

Another time, about ten of us travelled to Royal Ascot for the racing. We headed for the pub we normally use when we are near to the course. As we approached the door, it was obvious from the noise inside that some sort of argument was going on. Wally walked in first, but came flying back out at twice the speed. 'Fucking hell, Jim, someone's just lumped me.'

I walked in behind Wally and saw a man we knew from the area, a strong bory chavvy who was known as a rugby-playing, hard-drinking man who can have a row, waiting at the door with his fists ready. His name was Mark and he knew me, and dropped his arms and smiled. 'Hello, Jim.'

'It's too late for hellos,' I told him. 'That's my brother you've just hit.'

With that, Wally steamed straight into the man, who was almost a foot taller and six stone heavier than him. The whole place erupted. Drinkers scrambled for cover as the pub turned into a Wild West saloon. There were no guns but someone was squirting ammonia everywhere. It was chaos, and I must say I've never seen a brawl quite like it.

The police eventually came charging in the two doors, but I managed to slip out of another and mingle with the race crowds outside. Wally and this Mark mush got arrested. Wally protested that he had just walked into the pub and been attacked, which was true, but the police were sceptical. How come you are not marked? Where has all the blood on your shirt come from? Who hit you then? Wally said he didn't know who hit him. Mark's face was marked where Wally's rings had cut him up a bit, but he too didn't know who had hit him. Then the guvnor of the pub was wheeled in, but he couldn't remember seeing Wally or Mark in his pub. He told the police that he thought the people who started the fight are long gone.

---

Like a good travelling man, I upped sticks with my new family from Waltham Cross and ended up on a site in Edmonton. I started to use a pub nearby, the Cock Tavern. It was frequented by travellers from far and wide and was known as a place where you could get a game of cards or pool for money. Sometimes big money.

One night I got into a pool marathon with this mush and we were fairly evenly matched, but somehow I got myself £1,200 in his debt. Perhaps we weren't evenly matched after all. Twelve hundred pounds in those days was a lot of dosh. Twelve hundred pounds in *these* days is a lot of dosh, come to that. I challenged him to a double or quits and he agreed. I was about to save myself £1,200 or find that I owed a complete stranger £2,400 – the sort of money that people can get very funny over.

Needless to say, the punters in the Cock were pretty interested in the match and most of the drinkers who had lined up 50 pence pieces on the side of the pool table for a harmless game were not interested in interjecting.

'I'm on next,' said John Love, a traveller from Kent way, who I knew vaguely.

'No, John, I'm playing this man double or quits.'

'I don't care,' replies John, takes his coin from the table and crouches down and inserts the 50 pence bit in the slot.

The pub went quiet except for the sound of rolling pool balls as the coin releases the gate inside the table. I hit him twice as he straightened up and he staggered backwards. Before I could finish him off, he grabbed me around the neck and pulled me down to the floor with him. Everyone in the pub piled on top and quickly pulled us apart.

'Come on. I'll fight you now, John,' I growled as three or four men held my arms. Someone in the pub made the suggestion that we should fight tomorrow on the Edmonton site. It was dark now and we had both had a few beers. We agreed to reconvene the following morning.

I left the pub and went back to the site. I think the man I had been playing pool with was a bit shocked about what had just happened. He certainly never called after me, 'Hey! Hang on a minute. What about my £1,200?'

Back at the site, after the pub had closed, I carried on gambling, spinning the coin and playing headinams until three in the morning. I was so engrossed that the impending fight with Love had gone out of my mind. But I got up sharp in the morning, and took a mile-long run just to open the lungs up. I knew Johnny Love had a reputation, especially in Kent, as a good bare-knuckle fighter with more than his fair share of bottle. It was one of those names I had got to hear a lot about without really knowing him. I guessed it was the same for him. Looking back, it was inevitable that our paths would eventually cross.

---

Johnny Love arrives in the yard in style, pulling his truck up sharpish and jumping out with three of his mates in tow. He looks sleek and relaxed in a tight-fitting T-shirt showing his muscles, and tracksuit bottoms. John is a big, fit man around 6ft 3ins, weighing about 15 stone, and he bristles with confidence.

Wally is beside me to see fair play and John's uncle is there to do likewise. But unlike previous fights, there are not many other people around to witness the event. There hasn't really been enough time for the bush telegraph to crank into gear.

We come together in the middle of the ring and thud! It happens again. John fires his first one out and catches me on the jaw. Apparently I rocked and then swung back and toppled over like a skittle. I remember hitting the floor: the sensation of cold concrete on the back of my head, searing pain and being conscious of blood running down my neck and my back and soaking into my vest. If ever I wanted to stay down it is now, but I know I have to get to my feet. I couldn't live with being one-punched by the man from Kent.

I get up on to my feet unsteadily and Wally grabs my arm, maybe to straighten me out, maybe to stop Johnny coming in for the kill. His fingers probe around beneath my hairline. 'You can't go on, bruv,' he urges, and he's the last person on earth to tell you to stop 'You've got a hole in your skull I could get a ferret down.'

Thanks, Wally. Cheer me up. But I tell him I'm fine. I want to carry on. But Wally's not happy about it. I manage somehow to hold Johnny at bay as I get my head together, and then get into a rhythm of exchanging punches, but all the time I'm worried about my head wound. Blood is pissing out like a running tap and winding around my neck and down my front too. I hear someone whisper that it looks worse than it is. Wrong. It is worse than it looks.

As if that's not enough, John has got an excellent pointed jab that he drills into my face continually. I can remember that now like it was yesterday. Imagine a broom handle being prodded into your face time and time again and you're nearly there.

I'm fighting in a trance, on autopilot. I've lost track of time. Before I know it, we've been going for quarter of an hour, then half an hour and then three-quarters of an hour. We know this because we hear people say it to one another. Remember that the crowd are so close in you can smell the Old Holborn on their breath.

The next thing I remember is throwing out a wild haymaker that catches John and lays him clean out. The atmosphere is weird. Because there is hardly anyone around, there is no cheering from the crowd and I can hear them talking as well as their every sigh and gasp. It is almost like having a fight in someone's front room.

Johnny is out cold and not moving. His uncle bends down over him and splashes water onto his face, but there is still no reaction. This doesn't mean I've won the fight. There is no such thing as a knockout in bare-knuckle fighting, even if your opponent is spark out. When he finally comes round, he has the option of calling it a day or carrying on. As I said before, there is no trainer, no referee, no second ringside who can make the decision for you, look after you. It is down to you and your heart in bare-knuckle. At times, it is the loneliest place in the whole wide world.

Johnny Love finally sits up and looks around. Then he remembers where he is and gets to his feet. Wally tells me that we've been fighting for nearly an hour now, and I remember thinking, surely this can't go on for much longer? But as I thought he would, Johnny declares he's ready to carry on and we resume fighting.

I don't know if it is from the head wound or other cuts, but I am caked in blood. We've been fighting so long now that the blood from an hour ago has gone hard and dark on my chest, and the new blood runs over it. I can't see properly as it spills over my forehead into my eyes.

The longest bare-knuckle fight in the memory of most travellers was between Boxer Tom and John-John Stanley in a field in Watford back in 1972. The match lasted for two hours and 15 minutes, and for those who spectated, it remains the best ever fight. John-John was the victor on that occasion. The thought of this one going on anywhere nearly as long as that filled me with dread. I knew Johnny and me were both in a bad, bad way and unless something happened soon, one of us was going to be seriously injured or dead.

Wally stands in front of me at one point and I can see he is worried and upset. It makes me upset. 'Jimmy, are you all right?' I look back at him through a misty, bloody haze. We know each other so well. His look is saying: Bruv, it is no shame to give best. I'd rather you stop now than suffer some permanent damage, while my look is saying, Wally, I love you, I'm okay, it hasn't reached that stage yet.

The knockout has taken the sting from Johnny's punches. They have lost their relentless snap and I get to thinking that this is more about stamina now than anything else.

The fight goes on for another 45 minutes. That's a whole football match and a half of extra time, except there's two of us instead of 22, and we're face to face, trying to bash each other's brains out all of that time.

My eye sockets just keep filling up with blood and the swollen skin beneath is holding the blood in little reservoirs above my cheekbones. As quickly as I wipe them clean with the back of my hand, they fill up again. I can just about see Johnny through the blood, but it is like squinting through a misted-up window. My head feels scrambled, like bits have come loose somewhere inside and are rolling about. I feel sick. My legs are threatening to give and seem to be taking on a mind of their own. It's funny, I don't remember consciously deciding that I was going to stop, but I just did.

I lowered my hands and said, 'Johnny, I can't fight you no more. I can't see you, Johnny, to fight you.'

He looked at me, took my battered hands and shook them warmly. 'In that case we'll call it a draw, Jim.'

Johnny Love showed he was a true gentleman that day – a gypsy warrior and a man of honour, kindness and integrity. By rights he won the fight. I had given best. Johnny could have claimed the fight and no one, especially me, would have argued. He could also have simply finished me off and put me down, but instead he had taken my bruised hands in his and declared the fight a draw. Wally, though, was in a real state over the mess I was in and started to argue with Johnny. It shouldn't have happened, but it did. I understand why Wally was so emotional, but Love had behaved well and had been more than fair.

Before I knows it, they're fighting. Wally knocks him over three times and Johnny complains he's been hit low. They fight on for another ten minutes and then just stop and embrace each other.

It was wrong, because John had just felt me for nigh on two hours and then he's fighting someone fresh for another quarter of an hour. But it was an explosion of emotion on Wally's part. I think he thought I might die and he felt so helpless. I reckon Johnny saw this as well, and that was why after they calmed down they stopped and hugged each other.

Fingering the back of my head, I pulled out lumps of jelly-like blood where it had all congealed. The people around urged me to get up the hospital. But first I agreed to go to the pub, the Cart Overthrown, for the ritual of having a drink after the fight. I shouldn't have done, because I sicked my first pint straight back up and was unsteady on my feet like I was pissed. Someone phoned the wife and she came and picked me up and took me straight to the hospital. She had watched the fight and knew I was in a bad way. She hadn't wanted me to go to the pub in the first place, but I had assured her I was fine.

We sat in casualty for a couple of hours among the scalded arms, the injured footballers and the elderly with broken bones. Finally, a doctor and a nurse took me into a side room, gave me the once over and had me X-rayed. 'You have a double fracture of the skull, Mr Jones,' the doctor informed me. Jones was the first name that had come into my head on arrival.

'You say you did all this damage in a fall?' queried the nurse. The doctor looked at me over his little glasses knowingly. 'You must have fallen in front of the Flying Scotsman then.'

There is not a lot that can be done about a fractured skull. The doctor told me he wanted to keep me in overnight, as they liked to keep people with head injuries under observation, but I told him that would not be possible. They cleaned me up and reluctantly sent me home, telling me to lie still for a few days and then take it easy after that. They arranged for me to come back in a week, knowing that I wouldn't.

Lydia was calm, as always, when we got home, but I could tell she was worried and thinking that this could be a fight too far. She nursed me and cared for me as I spent most of the next week in bed. My eyes were in a terrible state. For weeks afterwards, I simply couldn't open them when I woke up. Lydia had to carefully put drops in and bathe them each morning before I was able to see. Fortunately, though, there was no permanent damage that I knew of, and within a couple of months I felt top again.

Johnny Love turned pro as a boxer not long after our marathon battle. I saw him next on the telly. It was one of them *Panorama*-type programmes, about whether boxing should be banned or not. Ever since Johnny Owen, the Welsh kid, died following a professional fight, there had been growing pressure to make boxers wear headgear, or even to ban boxing altogether.

To illustrate the dangers, they showed a clip of a fight between a big white guy and a big black guy. It showed them coming together at the start and the ref telling them what he expects of them. The black guy dances around a bit, and the white guy sort of stands there looking at him, like an old-fashioned bare-knuckle man. Then he unleashes a heavy left that explodes on the black man's chin and he crashes to the floor in a heap. Everyone jumps in the ring to attend to the man and it is clear that something is up. They are lifting up his eyelids and shining torches into his eyes but there is no response. The white man, who I realise is Johnny Love, looks on. Then the programme switches back to the studio and men in suits debate the dangers of gloved boxing. They say that the black fighter did come round 30 minutes later.

I met him next, two years or so after our fight, at a boxing show in Hayes where George Carman, another gypsy man, was fighting for the southern area title. John and his father-in-law, Henry Reynolds, with a man called Jack Barclay, came over and had drinks with Cousin Joe and me. We did talk of a rematch on Epsom Downs at the Derby meeting, but whilst many other people would have wanted it, I'm not sure either of us really wanted to go through it again. Wally met him too over the years, mainly down Kent way and especially in a particular Gravesend pub, and they got on well.

In the early 1990s, John began an affair with his sister-in-law. Families are everything with travellers and the implications of a relationship like this are even more momentous than they are in a gorger family. They were obviously deeply in love and couldn't see a way through. Knowing John, I suspect he couldn't bear to hurt those close to him. John and his lover were found lying next to each other, dead from gunshot wounds, in the beer garden of a pub in Orpington, Kent. A tragic end to the life of a great fighter and a great man.

# 10.

# COUSIN JOE

**JOE SMITH IS NOT ONLY** my cousin, but is also one of my best pals. All travellers are cousins, it sometimes seems, but the Frankhams, the Stockins, the Brazils and the Smiths are all closely linked. Joe's father was my father's nephew. He's 13 years younger than I am, but as soon as he could he was hanging around with us boys and enjoying the crack. His life has already taken some fascinating twists and turns. Joe takes us back to the beginning:

> I was born in Isleworth hospital to my parents Cissy and Aaron. I've got two brothers, Big John and Aaron, and three sisters, Mary, Maria and Louisa. Us boys all grew into big fellas – John is 24 stone, and me and Aaron are both six feet and solid.
>
> Like Jim, I travelled around with the family as a child and never really went to school, but there was a man called Jim Needle who came to the site and he very kindly taught me to read and write. We'd sit in the trailer and he'd show me the letters and make the sounds and I'd copy him. It was nice of him to take the time, but I always wanted to learn new things, to do things well. That's my way.
>
> Boxing has always been a big thing in our family. It was a

tradition, and when I was six I got taken down to Pitt House in Ewell, Surrey, and put on my first pair of gloves. Old Joe Taylor taught us the basics and took a great interest in our development. He had a bald head like a shiny bowling ball, and a jutting-out jaw. He wore a quilted green jersey all the time except for when we boxed at a show, and then he would wear his best blazer. Even at his age he had the movement of the skilful boxer he once was.

I enjoyed boxing as a sport, but I didn't like the fighting outside that many of the travelling boys participated in. To be truthful, as a young boy I got pushed around and bullied a bit.

About the same time that Joe Taylor was showing me how to put my guard up, my grandfather, Rymer, introduced me to golf. He had been a fighter in his time and a good one at that, but in later life he had taken to playing golf and allowed me to follow him around the courses pulling his trolley behind me. It was highly unusual then for gypsies to play golf – boxing has traditionally been the only mainstream sport that travellers have taken up, although in recent years there have been a couple of gypsy boys breaking through into professional football.

Rymer got into golf purely by chance. As a youth, he pulled up on a bit of land which was adjacent to a golf course. Him and his cousin, Nelson, watched as the men in their caps, pullovers and plus-fours played, and they soon fashioned clubs from wood and started to practise themselves. When no one was looking, they would sneak out on to the course and play one hole. One day, one of the members saw Nelson get a hole in one and was so impressed that he allowed them to continue to play on that one hole if no one else was around. So Grandad got me playing golf while, at the same time, old Joe Taylor was coaching me in boxing.

As soon as I could jump up into a truck I went to work with Dad, who acquired, bought and sold scrap metal. Dad was an honest man who didn't allow us to swear or chore. His only real vices were drink and gambling, although I wouldn't say he did these to much more excess than any other travelling man. We never went short, anyway, though much of my early years were spent waiting outside pubs and betting shops. But I didn't mind – it beat everything I had heared about school and I liked nothing better than to watch and study the characters who came in and out of the pubs.

Like I say, I didn't like fighting unless it was in a ring with gloves. I could see the point in that. So I steered clear of other kids who wanted to fight; sometimes I was teased and pushed around because of this. But when I was 13, I had a fight with a grown man and I have to say I enjoyed it. We had pulled into a petrol station, Mum and I, and like kids do, I was staring aimlessly at a man who had pulled into a nearby pump. I don't know what had happened in that man's life that day, but he flew into a rage and came at me, arms swinging like a windmill. Maybe he didn't like gypsies.

I was a kid and he was a man, and I was scared. I backed off from him but then I thought, if I'm going to get beat up anyway, I might as well hit back. Stepping back from him, I aimed a few punches at his head and suddenly it was him on the defensive. This inspired me, and I moved around him catching him with strong blows. I was so angry about what he had done that I wouldn't let up. Mum came running out of the shop and set about his head with her shoe. 'Leave him alone,' she cried, 'he's only 13.'

But by that time, it was matey who needed the protecting.

Grandad Rymer coached me on the golf all the time. He must have seen something in me to give over so much attention, and I loved playing.

I loved my grandfather. He was a gentle, patient man, and he slowly but surely developed my talent as a golfer, at the same time teaching me about life. We had so much time

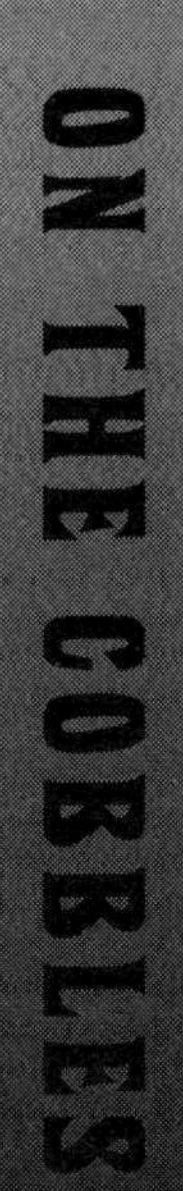

together alone walking between holes that he'd tell me about his life and about people and how to behave.

One day in a pub he challenged two old friends of his, who he knew played a bit of golf.

'My grandson, Joe, he's 12 years of age, he'll play you and I bet you he'll win.'

'We'll have some of that,' replied the men, and a friendly game was arranged for the following day.

That evening, as Rymer, Dad and I walked back from the pub where he had thrown down the challenge, he spoke to me. 'Joe, you could be a good boxer, I'm telling you, but take a look at me. Look at my nose, Joe, and my cauliflower ears. You don't need all that. You've got a talent, son, and that's golf. Promise me you'll practise and practise, don't take up the fighting, just golf, golf, golf, and you'll become a professional. I know you will. I won't be here to see it, Joe, but promise me you'll try and make it pro.'

'I promise, grandfather,' I said, 'and don't be silly, of course you'll be here to see it.' Dad and Rymer smiled down at me as I made my pledge.

The next day, I started to play three holes with these men and Rymer looked on proudly as I pushed in front on the first. Then I looked over and he was lying on the ground. We ran over to him and could see he was unconscious. My grandfather had had a massive heart attack and died on arrival at the hospital. Now, I take comfort he died like that. On the golf course, watching his young grandson playing golf, and with mercilessly little pain. When it's time for me to go, I wouldn't mind popping my clogs like that. But at the time it knocked me for six, him dying like that whilst watching me, and also because of what he had said the previous day, I believed he knew he was going to die. Now I'm not so sure. Older men say things like that.

I couldn't get the promise I had made to him out of my head

but, on the other hand, I felt bitter and angry that it had happened. Although I continued with the golf, I was also starting to get into more and more fights.

About a year later, when I was 14, I was in a pub in Hanworth with my brother Aaron. He got into an argument with the landlord, who was a 6ft 5in lump, and when he clumped my brother a big fight started. Aaron went down on the deck, so I felt I had to fight the publican myself. When I punched him it didn't seem to have much effect, but fortunately before he grabbed me Aaron was back up and sinking his fists into his face. The landlord went down this time and for good measure I stuck the boot into his crumpled body.

Another big man who was sitting on the other side of the pub rushed over and told me to leave it out, so I hit him with a combination and opened up the top of his eye. 'That's it, son, you are for it,' he roared, and he meant it. He was Ricky Sands, a former professional wrestler in his forties, who was well known in the area. He got me in a headlock and started to literally squeeze the life from me. All I could do was repeatedly bash away at his kidneys. Just as I started to feel faint and was about to black out, Sands collapsed to his knees and started gasping for breath. I jumped free and hit him with the hardest right-handers I could muster. I knew if the man got up I was dead meat. Me and Aaron left the pub with these two fat brutes lying sparko alongside each other.

Word later went round that Sands and the landlord were out for revenge and me and Aaron should expect a visit, when something quite nasty could happen. Dad had a friend called Ronnie Tompkins, who was a well-respected face around town, and he paid the two men a visit. Face up to it, he told them, you picked on a 19-year-old and a 14-year-old and you came unstuck. No more was said.

So, against my late grandfather's advice and wishes, I got to

bare-knuckle fighting. Rymer had been a top fighter in his time, but when he decided it was time to stop he did. Just like that. Rymer, his first cousin Wally and his brother Dido were all good boxers. They all turned pro and fought under the names Jack Daly, Dido Watson and Timmy Sullivan. I think their real names were fine, but in those days people tended to use a different fighting name.

The three of them toured the country fighting in the fairground booths and had many adventures along the way. Grandfather loved a wind-up, and he used to get Dido and Wally fighting – he got them fighting over cups of tea once, of all things. When Wally made the tea he would say, 'Lovely cup of tea that, Wally. Not too strong. Not too weak.' But when Dido made it he'd complain, 'Did you strain that tea through your socks, Dido? Can't you make tea like Wally?' and so on. As he planned, the two would soon be at each other's throats and they eventually settled the argument in a field.

It was the second fight they'd had in the space of a few weeks. The first had been through some stirring done by Posh, their pal, and afterwards Dido realised that the man who had caused all the trouble was sitting back laughing. He went to Posh's trailer and gave him a thrashing. Posh was a respected fighter, and some were surprised that Dido was able to deal with him so quickly.

Although grandfather would bewitch me with all these fighting stories, he was adamant that I shouldn't follow in his footsteps. They were for a different age, he said. A different time.

But did I listen? Throughout my teens and early twenties I had seven fights and won them all. The best and hardest was against a boy called Champ, the brother of Creamy, who my cousin Jimmy Stockins had fought many years before. Champ's wife had had an argument with one of my sisters, and a challenge was laid down.

We met up at the Cranford site. I had about 30 pals with me, although I must stress they had come to see what everyone knew was going to be a good fight, not to supply muscle, should there be a free-for-all. I also had my pal Alfie Summers as well as Jimmy Stockin, who had been nominated the fair play man. Champ, quite rightly, didn't want to kick off until his brother Creamy arrived. Creamy got there and he was with none other than my Uncle Ruffey, my Mum's brother, who was Creamy's close friend. Ruffey was a good man and it makes me sad when I think that he died last year. At least 300 people had assembled for the match and waited with great anticipation for the fight to begin.

Champ and me had a good fight, and Jimmy Stockin was scrupulously fair in his handling of it. I played the waiting game – that was my plan from the start. I paced myself and worked on Champ's body. I wasn't trying to damage him, I just knew that I could go on and on and on. Sooner or later Champ would get worn down or make a silly mistake.

We talked to one another all through the fight. On 40 minutes, Champ said: 'You'll never finish me with body shots, Joe.'

'Maybe I won't, but I'll keep trying,' I responded. By this time, I had cuts that would later require 14 stitches and a broken nose, but as I delivered another blow into his side, Champ gasped, 'You may be prepared to get beat up bad, but I'm not,' and gave best. That was the end of the fight. Forty-two minutes in all. My hands were black, literally black, from bruising. It was like I'd been wearing gloves after all. I could not see out of my eyes. The bone in my nose never fixed, and wobbles around to this day. Nevertheless, we all slipped off to the nearest pub and cracked open the champagne.

Another time I was drinking with my sisters. Some other travellers thought this strange for some reason, and called me a gay boy. I glared over and one of them, John Smith, jumped

up, pointed at me and said 'Do you want to fight? A man called Huggy Bear, due to his huge frame, told Smith to take me outside and beat me. I was about 15 and Smith was about 19. Huggy Bear was older still, already in his twenties. My sisters were screaming, and one of them got hit. I went berserk and floored one of the men, but four of them jumped on me and I ended up taking a pasting. I vowed to bide my time and to pay these men out one by one, especially Huggy Bear, who in my eyes was the ringleader.

John Smith was first, though. Christmas Day was good. Aaron and me drove over to his site and knocked on his trailer door, but his dad says he was out. He must be in the boozer scoffing his mince pies, we think, so we set off to the nearest pub. He wasn't there but, sure enough, he turned up and we gave him the choice of fighting Aaron or me. He decided I was a better bet. The fight went on for 20 minutes, but it was 20 minutes of him running. He had his guard up and did not hit me once. Aaron kept shouting, 'Hit him, Joe, he'll go!' but I'm not about to make a mistake.

But when I felt myself running out of puff – I had drunk four pints of lager and a brandy and lemonade whilst waiting for this joker – I decided to switch him off. A right to the head and then a cut up his ribs like a sword, and it was good night nurse, finito. Thanks for coming and fuck off!

Two years later, I ran into Mr H. Bear in the gambling ring on Epsom Downs. He was even bigger now – a good 20 stone, but I was older and more confident. 'Get your coat off,' I shouted, but he wouldn't.

I did have Jimmy Stockin standing beside me at the time, which probably influenced his reaction, so I didn't push it. When I did him, I didn't want to be accused of being mob-handed or him saying he wouldn't fight back because I had heavy people with me. But a couple of years later still, I saw him with a big entourage of his own at Barnet Fair, tucking into a plate of jellied eels. This time I knew that, whether he was up for it or not, it was time to get my revenge for what he had done to me when I was a kid.

I swapped my shoes for a friend's pair of trainers, knowing they would allow me to move around better when I started fighting, walked up to the counter and ordered a plate of eels. By this time, Huggy had seen me and as I swung around to take his fat head off, he ducked and smashed his fist into my chest. 'Make a ring. Make a ring,' cried the people around, who didn't think they were going to get a fight for the price of a plate of jellied eels, and we were off.

I smacked him in the teeth and his mouth filled with blood. Every punch I threw cut him and his face was springing leaks all over. I beat shit out of the cowardly bastard – punch after punch pounded into his fat face. I did him good and proper, and he knows and every one there knows what I mean. 'What's it all about?' he moaned, as if he didn't know. He looked up at me pathetically from the deck. I didn't want the spectators to think I was some sort of bully or a maniac, so I told them what he had done when I was little more than a child, and about my sister getting hurt.

It was like living two separate lives. At the same time as I was fighting with men in petrol stations, right through to when I got revenge on those bullies, I was pursuing my golf. At 12 years old, I had joined Twickenham golf club and on my 14th birthday I won the Richmond Handicap Open. My handicap at 14 was seven, and at 15 it was three.

Then I moved over to the Home Park club in Kingston, and soon won the London Junior Open, competing against 137 other boys. I received my trophy from Dennis Thatcher, whose wife was someone famous, I think.

At 16 I became the club champion for all age groups. This caused a stir. The newspapers took an interest and ran some pieces, and the BBC did a mini-documentary on me: 'Gypsy boy becomes golf champion' and all that stuff. That sort of thing seems to catch the public's imagination. There used to be a strip cartoon in one of the boy's comics years ago, about a gypsy boy who became a George Best-type footballer, but wouldn't wear football boots. Insisted on playing in his bare feet.

I won the Prince of Wales Challenge Cup in Sandwich, Kent, only to be told 20 minutes later that I was to return in six weeks for a play-off against the runner-up. It seems they didn't like the idea of a scruffy gypsy boy taking the title and the rules were bent against me. I lost the play-off. That was the first example that I remember of prejudice against me in the game. It was a novelty having a gypsy boy winning competitions at your club, but when the cameras and the newspapers had gone, there were some very jealous people left.

When I won the London Junior Open at Richmond, someone brought me over a tray of sandwiches, and my Dad, Big John and I shared them amongst ourselves. After I had received my trophy, Dad was passed a brown envelope. Here we go, he thinks, a nice little cheque for my boy Joe, but when he opened it he was surprised to see a bill for £4.25 for the sandwiches. He asked the bar steward what it was all about. Sandwiches are for players only, he was told, therefore he had to pay for what he and my brother had eaten. 'But my son and his two team-mates couldn't eat them all,' he protested, 'so we just ate what would have been left.' Four pound-odd is neither here nor there, but my Dad knew when someone was taking the piss and he refused to pay.

About a week later, I was called in to see the captain of the Home Park club. I was nervous because I thought they might chuck me out, but everyone said they wouldn't. You're the best thing that has happened to this club in years, they assured me, just take your slap on the wrist and get on with it.

I left the office in tears. The club did ask me to resign over this ridiculous, trumped-up incident. So I walked, rather than go through the humiliation of resigning. Len Roberts, an old pro and a gentleman, spoke up for me. He said: 'We have a kid here who respects everyone and wants to learn, and who could one day be a world champion, and we throw him out. Ridiculous!' He pointed out that another junior member only got a six-month suspension when his son was caught stealing from the golf shop. Mind you, he pointed out, he was the son of a policeman.

From then on, I went off the rails. Although I joined Hounslow Heath and represented the Middlesex under-21s, and still played well, my golf suffered and I started to lose it. My early potential seemed to disappear. I went on the drink, started fighting and robbing, and generally became a bad person.

I'm not saying the two things were connected – it was just coincidence that they happened at the same time. I didn't become a layabout because my golf suffered, nor did my golf suffer because I was a layabout. I was at the age when I didn't care. If the clubs didn't want me, then fuck them. That's how I felt.

That was my bad time. I moved around a great deal, upsetting a few people on the way. It got so bad that I knew I was heading for prison – or even for a bullet in the head.

I turned pro in desperation – my father's desperation, really. He knew I was ducking and diving. Mainly diving. He called and told me that a player called Alan Jarrett was going to Sweden to turn pro, and why didn't I go with him?

Why not? It got me out of the country and took my mind off things. I flew to Copenhagen and then took the boat to Malmo. I entered a Swedish golf tournament and played with Jesus Arruti and Johnny Carlsberg, but despite all the practice and the encouragement, I just couldn't cut it. I was useless.

Returning home, I went to see Dad and told him I had lost it. My day had gone and I was wasting everyone's time by keeping on trying. Dad told me that I mustn't give up – it was just a stage I was going through, and my talent couldn't have just disappeared. I could see he was really worried about me and thought that the golf was the only thing that could anchor me. As for my talent not having just disappeared – I wasn't convinced about that. Nevertheless, I went on Randy Fox's mini tour for golf pros, but played embarrassingly badly. I'd gone from scratch to playing like a 16 handicapper. Gypsy Joe Smith was getting worse, not better.

Then, through the drink and the depression, for the first time in years my grandad came back to me. It was just like he was there, Old Rymer, making me promise him I'd become a professional golfer. Well, I'd done that, but I wasn't one he'd be proud of. So I vowed to change my life, and I did. At Whittlebury Park in Northamptonshire, on the Hippo tour, I shot a four-under-par 68 and my game started improving.

I'm a professional attached to the course at Hounslow Heath now. My game is turning around and I am happy in my private life with my lovely wife and children. My boy is playing golf and I have high hopes for him. Two years ago, I just failed to qualify at Hillside for the Open at Birkdale. That was the year young Justin Rose, who I was playing alongside in the qualifiers, finished just two shots behind the leaders. I also played with Pierre Faulke in the final qualifier. I'm very patriotic, and the papers took an interest in me again at those qualifiers when I played with a St George's Cross dyed into my hair. They dubbed me England's John Daley.

At a practice match recently, I teed up next to Bernhard Langer, a childhood ambition. He was my hero, and I always told Mum and Dad that I wanted to be him and play with him. He had said some kind words of encouragement to me once when I was a baby playing the game and I never forgot it.

'Hello, Bernhard. It's me, Joey Smith, the gypsy kid. Remember?'

'I could not forget,' Langer said, beaming and gripping my hand. I looked over the barrier, and there were Mum and Dad smiling over. They were so happy and proud. I was so happy that I had to stop myself from crying.

We all knew then it was only going to get better. And that's where I am today – getting better all the time. I'm a professional golfer, and a gentleman on the course, and I always try my best. Grandad Rymer would be proud of me now, but I intend to go on and make him doubly proud. I *will* qualify for the Open.

There are more gypsies than you might think playing golf nowadays. I recently got a challenge from a man called Matty Brazil. He had seen my cousin and said he had heard about me, and believed that he could defeat me. Brazil is a common travelling name, but I didn't know of this chap, who came out of Cambridge. A game was arranged for £2,000, at a place called Barnhill.

I travelled up there at first light with my brother John in our battered old camper van, and went in to the hotel for a bit of breakfast. As I munched my scran, I heard a thick Romany accent behind me ordering food. Turning round, there was a smart man dressed in the best golfing gear. 'You must be Matty Brazil,' I said. He said he was, and we exchanged pleasantries.

Outside, he and his mate went to their cars – 100K of Merc between them. I glanced across towards my camper van but made no move towards it. One of my uncles who was a millionaire and could have at least evened up the status symbols a bit turned up, but he was in a battered old Mini. By now, between 50 and 100 travellers had gathered to watch the match. They had been told they would not be allowed entry to the bar after the game, which left a bad taste, but still no one kicked up.

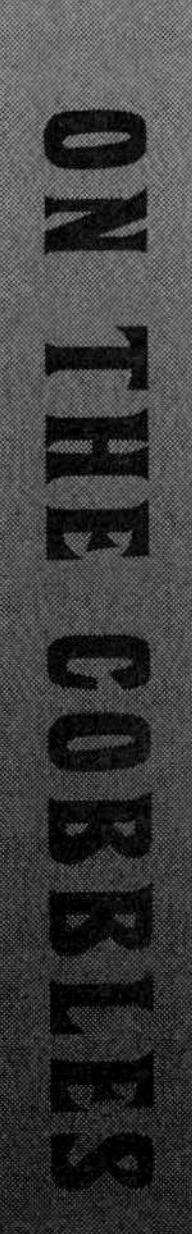

Matty spins a coin and wins to tee off. He hits his first shot 270 yards. I keep pace. By the sixth hole I'm one under par and Matty's level, but on the seventh I drop two shots and he's ahead. I'm playing well, but he's playing better. I can't believe I've never heard of this mush before, and I start suspecting he could be a ringer. I start speaking to him in Romany again, but there's no catching him out. He's a traveller for sure. Even Big Gilly, my caddy and a mean London taxi driver, gives me a look that says this ain't going to be easy, Joe.

By now, a considerable amount of gorgers had joined the spectators, and each shot was being eagerly anticipated. 'Come on, Cambridge,' urged Matt's contingent. And my lot, probably because they couldn't think of anything else, responded with, 'Come on, Oxford.'

On the next shot, Matty hits his ball and it sails into the trees. For some reason I feel my confidence rise and announce for everyone to hear, 'I'm aiming for the tree in the distance, near the pin.' I strike a 200-yard beauty. From then on, I push ahead, finishing with scores of 74 and 73, good tallies considering that the greens are in bad condition. More importantly, I end up beating Matt by ten shots. As good as his word, he pulls out a wad and pays me the prize-money.

'You're the best gypsy golfer I've ever seen,' he kindly said. 'It's a pleasure to play with a real pro.'

There you are then. King of the Gypsies – for a day, in golf, at least.

# 11.

# TWO WEDDINGS AND A FUNERAL



**THE JOHNNY LOVE FIGHT** was to be my last. I had a few rucks afterwards, but no more marathon classics. In fact, I consider Creamy, Kenny Symes and Johnny Love to be my only three 'real' fights. True contests. Those and the 180 amateur boxing matches I fought. But when you are pushing 30, bare-knuckle fighting is not a good idea. I've seen men carry on into their thirties, and even their forties, but they can be no match for hungry, young and fit men, however tough they once were. If they are not already, they end up becoming damaged.

One of the rucks I refer to was at a country and western day in Peterborough. We'd been on it all day, and me and some others were playing headinams with a man called Henry Francis. I was well drunk, and I shoved him in the way you do when you are pissed and playing around with each other in a lively game. I wasn't picking a fight or anything like it, but Henry saw it differently and put a few punches on me, opening up my face in the process.

He was less drunk than me and I had enough savvy to know this wasn't the time. I've said it before and I'll say it again – live for another day. So many people forget that. You wouldn't play football pissed or if you were whacked with tonsillitis. To me, fighting is the same. If you possibly can, don't put more against you than there already is.

I went back to my trailer and cleaned up, then I went round to where I was told that Henry was to fight me in the morning. But Henry had gone. Pulled off the site, back to the north of England, where he came from. 'He didn't know who you were, Jim,' pleaded someone who knew him.

'Too bad, tell him I'm coming to find him.'

I knew he'd be at the Doncaster St Leger meeting. That was his stamping ground and the St Leger was the northern travellers' Derby. I made sure I put the word around that I was coming. We trekked up there in a convoy of motors, about 30 of us. That's a lot of men. But when you are going on to another man's patch, especially to do violence, you have to prepare for the worst. I've never been shot or shot at, but I know plenty that have. We fight mainly with our fists – you rarely hear of travellers knifing or glassing one another – but if a row is personal, about family, and is serious, then sometimes, sadly, knives and even guns have been involved.

When we pulled up near the course, it was like the wagon train had arrived – seven or eight cars, full of big strapping blokes climbing out. I saw Henry's father and brother, and they said they didn't know where he was. 'He didn't know it was you, Jim,' one told me. No one touched the dad or the brother: it wasn't their row.

We pressed on to the pub where we were pretty sure Henry and his boys would be. We split into two groups, and burst in both doors to stop anyone bolting. The pub went deadly silent as we scanned the faces for Henry. Fortunately for him, and maybe for me in the long run, he wasn't there. We went back to his site and sat in the cars for three or four hours, but Henry was nowhere to be seen. Eventually, we headed via a few pubs back to the south of England. I never saw the man again.

I had other interests now. We stayed at Edmonton for three years and in this time our second child, Jolene, was born. I was happy with my family and friends – at that time mainly Tommy, Billy and Archie Brown who all lived on the site.

Then we moved back to West Drayton and our third child, another daughter, comes along. We call her Elizabeth. My work is regular as I build up a little roofing and building business.

I'm still having a drink, but I'm not on the piss big-time. The only time I have a real lash-up is at weddings and funerals. Travellers love to celebrate an occasion, be it wetting a newborn baby's head, a wedding or even a funeral. We do it in style, although sometimes these events can end up in massive brawls, at weddings particularly – when two families come together. If there has ever been bad blood – even if it was years before – it seems to float to the top on these occasions.

I remember going to a wedding years ago with my sisters, Wally, Mum and Dad. Actually, the family had been invited to two weddings on the same day, so Dad decided we'd spend a couple of hours at one reception in Aldershot and then move on to the second party in Staines to see the night out.

Gypsy weddings are the same as anyone else's, inasmuch as we have a ceremony in a church or a registry office, and then all decamp to a big party in a hall or a pub. But we see the wedding as a good opportunity to get our best clobber out and sling on the gold, and we like to make a good entrance in a new, shiny four-wheel drive or a big old Mercedes motor. The girls always look a treat and plaster on some make-up, and the kids are dressed up as pretty as dolls.

As we arrived at the reception in Aldershot and Dad was parking up, we could see that a fully fledged fight was in progress. Outside the hall entrance, people were running around landing punches on one another. Buttonhole flowers were flying off lapels as men wrestled each other to the floor, and the women were screaming, scratching and ripping the hair out of one another. Little children holding bottles of Coca-Cola sucked on their straws and watched calmly, as their mums and dads tried to disfigure each other.

There was a man lying on the ground, and I noticed he sneaked open an eye and then shut it again. He was hoping that by playing dead he'd be left alone, but soon jumped to his feet and ran when he was booted in the stomach and realised there was worse to come.

'It's a bit too quiet here for me,' commented Dad, and we all got back into the motor and headed off Staines way.

No disrespect to our women, but sometimes it was them that

started the fights, intentionally or unintentionally. Like I said, they'd have their best gold on, short mini-skirts, high-heeled shoes and maybe a slice of cleavage showing. It was hard for a man not to take a lingering look now and then. But God forbid that his missus should see him. If she's a fiery lady, she may well walk up to the lady who is being looked at and smack her straight in the lipstick. Then it's all off. And that's nothing to what will happen to the old man when they get home. Whoremongering, the women call it.

If gypsy men can be characterised by their willingness to fight at the drop of a hat, the women, many of them, can be characterised by their extreme jealousy – much of the time unfounded.

However, when there is some substance to their jealousy, it can lead to tragedies and violence. That is what happened to my good friend Mark Ripley. Mark was the man who ensured fair play when I fought Creamy all those years ago, and was there again for the Kenny Symes fight. He was respected and feared in equal measure by gypsies and gorgers alike. It seems that Mark was playing around and his wife found out. He was drinking in a pub over Croydon way one day, when she walked in and shot him dead. I don't know the ins and outs of it, and I don't want to, but I still feel gutted to this day at how Mark's life was ended. His wife was treated sympathetically by the judge and, although she was brought to trial, she walked. I don't know of anyone who has seen her since.

Back to the two weddings. If someone had said there would be trouble at one of the dos that night we would all have plumped for the Staines one, as it was one of the Reed boys who was getting married. The Reed boys were wild, and could all have a fight – Adam especially. Johnny Frankham told me about a fight he refereed between Adam, when he was only about 17, and Johnny Brazil. The fight was over who was the best. Stupid reason, really, but there you go.

Johnny Bloomfield, who has trained some top fighters in his time, maintains that Johnny Brazil was one of the best men he ever worked with, and Adam, well, Adam was wild, as I say. The match was held in the back garden of a council house but was nevertheless well attended.

Adam nutted Johnny Brazil at the beginning and Johnny Frankham had to warn him about fair play. The fight proper only lasted ten to 15 minutes, but Johnny says it was one of the best he has ever witnessed. Brazil's famed killer punch opened up Adam's face, but Adam was just too strong and in the end Johnny Brazil went down and gave best.

I, too, had a fight with Adam, up on Epsom Downs. Because I had a name, every up-and-coming young gypsy fighter wanted to take a pop at me and this was a problem for a while. Adam came to my trailer and offered me out. It was no fight, really. I hit him a few times, and he went down. His mate, Billy Appleton, stepped forward and I did him too. Billy surrendered. For good measure, Wally had a fight with Adam's brother, David, and came out on top.

I liked Adam and admired his spirit and I was as sad as the next man when he died not too long after. I can't recall the exact details, but I think Adam was on the trot, or with someone on the trot, or maybe they were due to return to prison from home leave – something like that – and they somehow wrapped the motor they were in around a tree. The strange thing was that they were said to be on a long stretch of road and this was the only tree for miles. Sadly, Billy Appleton died too some years later – from a heart attack, I believe.

This Reed wedding, though, was going fine, everyone happily chatting and eating chicken drumsticks off paper plates. The men had unbuttoned their suit jackets to reveal pot bellies restrained by braces as they swigged on bottles of brown ale. The little kids out on the dance floor ran between the legs of couples as they smooched to Elvis numbers.

Suddenly – bang – it goes off. One of the Reed boys hits a guest and somewhere along the line a glass gets smashed over someone's head. All hell breaks loose. The kids scurry off into an adjoining room. Someone lifts a table up and the food slides down the tablecloth and falls off the end on to the floor. Chairs are flying. The DJ gives up and starts to pack his records away rapidly. A gypsy wedding without a brawl is like a bare-knuckle fight without blood – almost unheard of.

Cousin Joe recalls a wedding he attended as a kid. A fight had started between his uncle, Freddie French, who in his younger days was one of the best fighting men to come out of Kent, and four men, who had surrounded him. Joe's auntie grabbed a broom from the corner of the hall and prodded one of the men in the back, then when he turned around she smashed the end of the broom into his face. Freddie then hit one of the remaining three, but auntie got carried away when she went for the next one, missed, and almost laid poor Freddie out with the full force of the broom head. Joe said the ensuing fight was like a Wild West bar-room brawl, and he remembers standing there watching it all as he nibbled on a sausage roll. The free-for-all eventually ran out of steam, and everyone stood around nursing bruises and wondering how it started in the first place. Backs were slapped, hands were shook and the party shuddered back into gear.

Even at funerals it can go off. It shouldn't do, but sometimes it happens. Emotions are running high and travelling people don't hold in their emotions too well. We say what we think to each other. If we have a grievance we don't nurse it or keep it buried, we have to get it out in the open. That's how it is.

Someone started on me at a funeral once, but I managed to keep a lid on it. Had it been anywhere else, I would have slaughtered the man. It was at Johnny Brazil's Uncle Bill's funeral, and I was standing on my own when this man, who looked 20 years my senior, came up to me and growled, 'You stay your side of the fence, Stockin, and I'll stay mine,' and then strode off into the church.

I was baffled more than anything. I'd never set eyes on the mush. In the church, I copped him looking over the top of his hymn book at me with that don't-fuck-with-me, you'll-regret-it kind of stare. It unsettled me, I have to admit. When a complete stranger seems to know who you are and wants to rip your head off, it is kind of worrying.

In the pub, at the wake, Georgie Carman walked up to me and said he'd heard what the fella said. 'If it goes off, Jim, I'm with you all the way.' Good old George. He's a good bloke and has been a top fighter in his time – but who the fuck was this man? He didn't hang around the pub and was soon gone, but I had to find out what it was all about.

Eventually, someone told me the chavvy's name. He was known as Jim Smith, and came from down Chichester way. I was still none the wiser, though, so I got his phone number and called him up the next day.

'Thought you might call, Stockin,' he says.

'What's all this about?'

'You don't remember, then?'

'No, pal, I've never met youse in my life.' Apparently I had. He reckons he had a row with Wally and me at a trotting match once. Well, it must have been a minor row and it must have been a very long time ago, because neither Wally nor me could recall anything about it.

'I want to settle this once and for all,' Jim Smith goes on. 'I challenge you to a fight on the cobbles.'

'You're on.' This idiot was getting on my nerves now. I swear I had no row with him that I could remember, so I couldn't apologise for it even if I had wanted to. He was determined to fight me. We duly arranged to meet at Guildford in Surrey, a town we agreed was halfway between us both.

We drove down there about ten-handed – we couldn't be sure how many this mush Smith was going to bring. Something just didn't add up and I was wary. Ken Stanley, my mates Dave and John, and the Browns were among the men with me that morning.

We didn't have too long to wait at our agreed meeting place, a pub on the old London Road, as Jim Smith soon arrived in a battered old pick-up truck and just he and two younger men got out. 'These are my two kid brothers,' said Jim and I nodded over at them. I could see they were much fitter than their older brother. On looking at him, I noticed that not only was he not very fit, but also that he didn't really want to be doing this. His body language was nervous and the growling stance he had at the wedding had disappeared. To be honest, I felt a bit sorry for him. He was a good few years older than I was and I knew I was going to batter him.

'You sure one of you two boys don't want to fight me instead?' I asked, addressing the brothers.

‘No, mate. Jim’s the best fighting man in our family,’ they replied surely. We all got back into our cars and were told to follow the Smiths’ wagon. They led us down a few country lanes and then up a track, where we parked up.

Jim Smith came and faced me. ‘Do you mind if I wear these?’

He was holding up a pair of thin black leather gloves, the sort of poncy things you’d see Leslie Phillips wearing in an open-topped E-type Jag, in one of those old ‘Doctor’ films. I don’t mind. This bloke is a real weirdo. I notice as he tugs the gloves down his fingers that he’s trembling a bit.

We shape up and he makes no real attempt at putting up a serious guard. I plant two or three good punches in his face, and he goes down in a heap on the muddy field. He’s not knocked out and he just sits there for several seconds looking down at the ground. Like he’s going to get some inspiration. Then he gets to his feet and puts his fists up to signify he wants to carry on. It crosses my mind that the bloke might be the bare-knuckle equivalent of a pool hall hustler. But what would be the point? There is no money riding on the fight. There ain’t going to be no double or quits. I put one foot forward, bring up the right and hook him. He’s down again, but this time I’ve switched him off.

I look around and can see that everyone is a bit embarrassed. I’ve just fought a man in his mid-to-late forties who should have known better. He wasn’t even in good shape for a man that age, and he didn’t throw one punch. His brothers bring him round and Jim Smith leaps across to me and shakes me by the hand. ‘The best man won,’ he smiles, and now he seems perfectly relaxed and happy. I don’t like to point out that there was only one man fighting.

‘I think we need a drink, eh Jim?’ Not really. I hadn’t exerted much more effort than swatting a fly, but this fella wanted to and I could see there was no harm in him. Us lot and Jim Smith and his brothers had a good drink in a country pub, then headed off to our homes.

I still couldn’t work out what it was all about, whether Wally and I had ever really offended him. Someone said to me that he probably just wanted to boost his reputation back where he stayed by saying he had challenged and fought Jimmy Stockin. Who knows? But coming home, I couldn't help thinking there was something about him lying there on the grass that was familiar, and then I remembered. A trotting match, an argument, me, Wally and Boxer Tom. That was down Portsmouth way. Jim Smith must have been one of the men Wally and me floored that day all those years before.

Reputations, though, are funny things. I know Wally and me both had one – much of it totally false. I've heard men tell stories about me and Wally, not knowing who I was, about how we fought pubs full of nutcases or how we had beaten Frank Bruno or some other big name in a sparring match. That sort of thing.

On the subject of reputations, Johnny Frankham told me a story about an incident that happened to him only recently. Johnny was having a quiet game of darts in his local pub, when this travelling man came in. He'd been in the pub before and seemed a nice enough geezer, but he did have a lot of trap. There was nowhere he hadn't been, nothing he hadn't done, and no one he didn't know. This night, he got to telling the other locals how he had been a good fighting man in his time. 'I beat that Johnny Frankham, you know.'

'Johnny Frankham?' queried one the drinkers, looking over at Johnny sitting quietly at the bar.

'Yeah. The one they called Gypsy Johnny Frankham, who was a boxing champion and all that.'

'Beat him easy, did you?' They were having fun with the man now. Johnny still hadn't looked up from his paper.

'Nah, it was a tough fight. He was a good little rower that Frankham. But I did him in the end.' The bloke leading the wind-up called over to Johnny.

'Did you hear that, Johnny? This man says you gave him a tough fight. By the way,' he turns back to the man, 'that is Johnny Frankham sitting over there at the bar.'

The colour drained from the man's face, although Johnny smiled over at him in a reassuring way. 'That ain't the Johnny Frankham I fought! The man I fought must have been lying,' he finally stammered. Johnny saved the man's embarrassment by buying him a drink.

Johnny Frankham once knocked out the legendary heavyweight world champion, Muhammed Ali. Did you know that? Well, he possesses a photo of himself standing over the heavyweight champion of the world as he lies on the canvas with his arms outstretched. Ali was at the Albert Hall to fight someone, and before the match some other English boxers jumped in the ring for an exhibition spar with him. Being the showman and the great sport that he was, Muhammed feigned being knocked out by Johnny and the others to allow a great photo opportunity.

---

Back on the West Drayton site my wife gives birth to our fourth child, and I'm delighted when I learn it's a boy. I love my girls and would die for them, but I thought perhaps I'd never have a boy. Us gypsies always want a son to carry on the family line. We christened him Jimmy Dean Rocky Marciano and I get straight down the bookie's and bet that Jimmy Dean will win a British boxing title before he is 25 years old. The bookie tells the papers about the bet, and the next thing I know *The Sun* are round. They photograph him with this pair of boxing gloves on his little fat baby arms and put the story and the picture in the paper.

I'm so proud now, with my son and my girls, and feel complete at last. All the happy memories of Dad come flooding back and I only wish he could have seen his grandson.

We wet the baby's head in style. I was on the missing list for three days.

But soon it was time to move on from the West Drayton site. I had no choice in the matter as an eviction order was placed on me, and I decided to move my own self before the council towed my home away. I'm having no fucker pulling and pushing my home around. Imagine how you'd feel if someone on the council took a dislike to you, came along with a dirty great forklift, lifted your house up and drove off with it to try and find somewhere else to put it down.

We were happy at West Drayton. I was the guvnor of the site, and that is where the problems started. When I say the guvnor, I don't mean in a gangster sort of way. People came to me to settle disputes and ask advice, and I'd help them out if I could. There's normally a guvnor on most sites: someone who is respected and can keep the peace. I decided who came on and when. Didn't allow any riffraff on the site. We had a good bunch of families and I was determined to keep it that way. But it was a council-run site, and they employed a warden.

Inevitably, the warden and me were soon at loggerheads. He didn't like the fact that no one listened to him and would only do something if I said it was okay. He complained that I undermined him. Of course, that is exactly what I did – he was a fucking idiot. He wasn't even a traveller, so he didn't understand us. It was him or me. So he went behind my back and set the wheels in motion to have me evicted. Ridiculously, he claimed I tried to run him over in my truck. I did pretend to once. I stared maniacally at him out of my windscreen, gripped the steering wheel and shouted 'Out the way!' but the truck was stationary and the engine wasn't even switched on. I did it to annoy him. If I had wanted to hurt the silly old bastard, I would have done.

After I left, I heard the warden had a hard time. He couldn't control the residents and even though he was taking a few quid in backhanders for prime pitches, his life was made a misery. He told one of my pals that he wished I'd never gone.

From there we went to Swallow Street in Iver, where an old disused yard had been compulsorily purchased by the council, so I figured we'd be left alone there for a while. That's the problems travellers face: they don't like us when we travel, and they like us even less when we stop. As if to underline this, we were moved on quickly even though our presence interfered with no one and there was no sign of any redeveloping happening any time soon.

We ended up in a shithole called Baleswood Lane. It was a rough piece of land, alive with rats. These rodents activate an ingrained fear in gypsies. I suppose that over the centuries we've lived too close to them for comfort. When we were kids it wasn't the bogeyman that would get us, it was the rats.

The rats at Baleswood Lane clearly had a good amount of food available to them, because they had grown to the size of fucking otters. Even the dog had given up or was too frightened to chase them. They'd scramble around him as if he wasn't there. 'We can't bring the kids up like this,' said the missus finally. 'I'm putting our name down on the council list.'

I had mixed feelings about this but she had a point. It had become harder and harder to travel. All the gypsies' traditional stopping places had gone, so when we did stop it was in places where we were stopping 'illegally'. And no sooner had we uncoupled the trailer than the men in suits were upon us with their writs and orders. And then the braver local residents would traipse over to challenge us, fearing we might have our eyes on kidnapping their children or shitting in their garden sheds. It was wearing us down and more and more travellers were giving up their way of life to take a council house. I sometimes thought that the government built the M25 so that they could put us all on it and make us just keep going round and round.

Eventually, we got a house, abandoned life in the trailer and moved in. I couldn't help remembering how it had affected Dad some 30 years earlier – it had made him miserable and ill. It was the end of an era in my life, and I knew it would be much harder than it had been for Dad to revert to my previous way of life, should it not work out. But I was glad to get away from the rats and the piles of rubbish that the local residents dumped in Baleswood Lane. They thought that because we were gypsies we could do with their rubbish and filth as well as our own. The day we moved in, as we put our photos of the children up and laid out our best china, I knew that this was the first day of the rest of my life.

# 12.

# THE PEACEFUL LIFE



**WE DID SETTLE DOWN TO LIFE** with a roof over our heads. I even got used to lying back in a bath full of hot water, which at first seemed the oddest of gorger domestic routines. You get in a bath full of water, wash all the dirt and grime off your own self and then soak in that same filthy, still water for half an hour. That habit struck me in the same way as our habits may have done you when I talked earlier about how, when we were on the road, our lavatories were behind hedges in fields. Like a cat, we'd kick a bit of dirt over a turd we'd just laid. It is not a matter of being dirty – just different ways of living.

We even share our house with a dog now. Not in a million years would travellers allow dogs or cats inside their trailers. We loved them, but they were dirty and smelt, and could not share our living space; we felt exactly the same about that as a gorger family would about allowing a dirty old badger to nose in the front door and curl up in front of the television.

We've got toilets now with chains to pull or levers to push, and with a whoosh and a bit of magic your lavatory is all clean, looking up at you for the next visitor. Sometimes I watch my Jimmy Dean as he comes out the toilet, washes his hands, goes to the refrigerator and swigs back some Coca-Cola. He will never know life on the road I doubt, never know a Toucher who goes out and bags the family's dinner with a catapult. He will never stand by an old fire on a huge and rambling site on Epsom Downs, where the old gypsy men tell stories from yesteryear.

Maybe for Jimmy Dean, and the next generation, this is a good thing. Because to be a gypsy now is to be a criminal. Over the course of my lifetime, the travelling way of life has been criminalised and I guess that my generation were the last to live like our forefathers had for centuries. That is sad.

I saw something on the telly recently. It was about a little shop which had been preserved exactly as it was when the owner had died in the 1950s, and it had become a tourist attraction. People flocked from all over to see the old-fashioned scales and the long-forgotten boxes of soap powder and sweets from their childhood. I think that is what the gypsies had. Whilst the rest of the world was changing from the Middle Ages onwards, the gypsies carried on as ever, maybe lagging a century behind the rest of society.

When the Industrial Revolution came and people abandoned age-old working practices to work in factories, the gypsies continued to sharpen knives and make baskets, earning their living in simple, traditional rural ways. When the motor car arrived, gypsies continued, for many years, to use the horse as their main mode of transport. Therefore, we provided a window on the past. We also appealed to the gypsy in every one. We were doing what they thought they might like to do and, indeed, many did do for a couple of weeks a year with their caravans and travelling holidays. Perhaps there was jealousy there? Seeing tribes of mainly happy people touring around, enjoying the countryside, not beholden to a mortgage or a large corporate employer, not knowing what was going to happen next. Living as their ancestors had centuries before.

Whatever the problem really was, attitudes hardened in the 1960s and from then on there has been a concerted effort to stamp out our way of life and force us to surrender our culture in exchange for a cease-fire on the harassment front.

Sad to say, I think they have succeeded. There are almost no English gypsies left on the road. The traditional stopping places have all gone. The disused airfields are now home to thousands of identical-looking houses. Farmers, even the ones who want us, are prevented by law from allowing us to pull up on their land. The English travellers have nearly all taken houses or live on permanent sites.

When we first started living in houses, travellers would put cartwheels on their outside walls, or have stone statues of horses in the garden as a sign of their heritage. But no amount of signs can alter the fact that English travellers are no longer travelling. The ones you see on the move nowadays are mainly the Irish travellers, who are a whole different race. They are from different stock, speak a different language and live a different way. To say that the Irish travellers and the British gypsies are one, is the same as lumping West Indians and Asians as a single race.

Now, because we have been forced to live in the same way as everyone else, the problems that dog the rest of society have started to catch up with us as well. Take drugs. Gypsies resisted the taking of drugs even when it became a pastime of the young masses from the 1970s onward. We weren't anti-drugs, there was just no need for them in our lives. They had nothing to offer travelling folk. But slowly, they have seeped in to our culture amongst our young. Now, I've snorted and like a puff – to class puff as a dangerous drug is a joke. I used it in prison where, believe me, it is the norm and generally encouraged, because it mellows you out. Helps you get through the sentence. If the prison authorities were honest, they'd like to make it compulsory let alone legalise it! But it is the heroin that worries me.

I said earlier that we don't steal from one each other. People's trailers did not get burgled, full stop. Our moral code was a strong one, but now even that has changed. Not so long ago, a relative of Wally's stole some fine china belonging to him. He and his mates were young heroin addicts and Wally and me went after them to teach them a lesson and get the china back. Some hope! My point is, they knew that if Wally and me came after them it was serious trouble, but they still did it. They still did it, because heroin removes everything – morals, sense and fear. When we finally caught up with them, the main culprit did rediscover his fear momentarily and jumped clean out of a first-floor window.

Crime is everywhere now. Not that long ago, I was approached by two fellas outside a club in Tottenham. They had seen the chain with a pair of boxing gloves on it that I sometimes wore around my neck. They asked to look at it, but I knew they would give it a tug and that would be it, so I told them to fuck off. One pulled a knife and they tried to back me up. 'Put that away, pal,' I warned, 'because I will get it off you and push it so far up your arse it'll come through your eye socket.' I walked towards them and, fortunately, on this occasion, they ran away.

Only recently someone read me an article in the *Daily Mail* which said that the police were launching a drive to recruit gypsies. Now, how true this is I can't say, and even if it is, I can't see many travelling boys queuing up to join. However, even the police pretending they want us and recognising us as an ethnic minority is a step forward.

Things change and I accept that. Life was good in our house and the kids even started going to school. What happened next, though, wasn't meant to. In terms of this book, it should have occured six chapters ago, but that is what happens with me – life is full of surprises.

I was working and doing okay. Me and my nephew were doing small building jobs and a bit of roofing and guttering work. We'd drive around and spot a roof with some tiles missing, then knock on the door and point it out to the owner. We'd tell them we were working in the area, and ask if he or she would like us to give an estimate on the repair. Half the time, the owner said yes, and we'd do it. The other half would view us with suspicion, even contempt. Often though, after we had started work, another neighbour would stroll over and ask us to attend to their tiles or gutters too. That's how it worked. We had many happy and satisfied customers.

This day, we were looking up at a roof with a few tiles missing, and some dodgy-looking ridges. 'They're dangerous, they are, missus,' I rubbed my chin like my old Dad did, 'a strong wind could blow them off and they might land anywhere. Look, we've got the ladders out. Why don't you let us put 'em right for you?' She was okay about it and we set to work.

Meanwhile, on the other side of the road, the police had turned up where a domestic row was in full swing. My nephew and me sat on the roof and drew on a roll-up as we watched the goings-on across the street. The old lady next door to the neighbours from hell engaged the police in conversation as they prepared to leave the house. Next thing, I noticed her pointing at us two on the roof, and the two policemen peering up at us. One of them strolled across and shouted at us to come down. What have I done now? Okay, I know I've been on the roof, taking in the sun and watching the entertainment, but that ain't a crime, surely? What are they going to charge me with – gross laziness? 'The lady across the road tells me you're ripping her elderly neighbour off,' he announces.

'How can we be ripping anyone off?' I protest 'We haven't even agreed a price with the lady yet.' He makes us take our ladders down and tells us to follow him to the police station. We are interviewed and then released on police bail.

I knew we wouldn't be charged, because we had done nothing wrong. It was harassment from the gavvers and we were used to it. It's annoying, but you learn to live with it. We were lippy with them because we were angry, and that annoyed them more. We shouldn't have done that, because in the end the gavvers always win.

Next day I'm back out, this time with my pal Skunk, and over the next few weeks we turn over a regular bit of work. I forget about the gavvers.

Some weeks later, we get a call from a lady over in Staines who tells me her mum and dad have just bought her a house, and friends of hers gave her our number because we did good work for them some time ago. Could we pop over and have a look? Sure we could.

Skunk goes up the ladder and brings down a broken roof tile. He tells the woman her ridge tiles are loose and dangerous, and we agree a price of £320 to put it right. I grab a bucket to fill with water so I can knock up some sand and cement. She tells me her water isn't working and I should go next door for it, which strikes me as weird. Then an Old Bill car screeches up, and a bunch of them jump out and arrest Skunk and me. They claim to have been watching us for a couple of months. They take both of us back to our houses and seize a bankbook of mine. We are both charged with deception. This is all I need.

We are bailed straightaway, and I make the mistake of believing that this is just further hassle from the Old Bill because they don't want us working their patch. They say they have evidence from six householders that our eventual charge was considerably more than our estimate – I think they put the total amount of overcharging at £1,500. Significantly, there are no charges of demanding money with menaces, threats or the like. If they really have been tailing us for weeks, we must have done 50 houses at least in that time. So six householders, when pressed by police, have said that we charged them more than we agreed. What about the other 44?

Skunk and I decided to plead guilty at our court case, nearly a year after our arrest. We pleaded guilty because, technically, maybe we did deceive – sometimes our final price *was* more than our estimate – and we believed, and were advised, that by pleading guilty we were likely to be treated far more leniently. How wrong we were. Skunk got 15 months and they hit me with two and a half years. We were shell shocked.

Poor old Skunk. He is such a lovely man. Like me, he lost his father violently: his dad was the landlord of one of the pubs hit in the IRA bombing of Birmingham in the '70s. I considered myself a family man who scratched a reasonable living. Some murderers don't get much more than I did. In my dad's case, the murderers got considerably less. Prison, I had mistakenly believed, was in the past.

What about the people we deceived? What we did was, for example, agree a price of £300, but once we were on the roof we might discover more that needed doing, or that the job was more work than we envisaged. We would then tell the owner that actually the bill came to more than our estimate. It *is* an estimate, after all. Estimate means guess, doesn't it? Okay, so this is not strictly ethical. But is two and a half years in jail ethical?

I took the two and a half on the chin. But why was I the only mush in jail for this crime? The bloke in the cell next to me was a bank robber, the one next to him a drug dealer, and the one after that a violent pub brawler who almost killed two men. In the whole prison I couldn't find one garage owner or mortgage salesman.

How often have you taken your car into a garage, got an estimate and gone to collect it a day or two later only to discover that the bill is half again the estimate: 'Sorry about that, sir, but your overhead cam safety nuts were damaged and your oil pipe was faulty so we had to fix all that while we were in there.' No one argues, they probably have a moan but they accept it. He can't be a criminal, he wears a suit.

And what about all those people who were sold endowment mortgages in the 1980s? They're writing to them now, saying sorry, but we need another £10,000 off you to ensure the endowment can pay off the mortgage.

And it goes on. From builders to plumbers to big companies to mini-cab drivers. It is everywhere. Half the people in the Yellow Pages use similar business practices. But the gypsy boys do it, and they get two and a half years. Either I'm doing too much time here, or everyone else is doing too little. If you need a garden wall built and get five quotes, you would probably take the lowest. But would those other four builders get charged with attempted deception? I think not.

---

The prison system had changed a bit since I was last in. I started in Wormwood Scrubs, then got sent over to a new one near Hemel Hempstead called The Mount, and finished up at Send, near Guildford in Surrey. Most of the inmates seemed younger at the first two nicks, or was it just me getting older? Prison is a young man's game. When you are young, you can do your bird knowing that the rest of your life is in front of you – the rebuilding you have to do when you come out isn't a huge problem. When you're older, though, you realise that you ain't living for ever. You know that two years in your children's life is an enormous space of time. You know that you're not getting those two years back. I decided that, as before, I would keep my head down, do my bird and get out. But it was easier said than done.

Because it's such a small, sad world in prison, little things get blown out of all proportion. I was sitting in the dinner room one day when this fella, a bit of a face from Manchester, looked over and told me I had a haircut like Frankenstein's monster. 'With a face like yours,' I said, 'you could be his fucking double.' Pathetic, I know. But he had made me look a fool in front of a room full of people, and there was no need for it. Before that day, we had not exchanged a glance or spoken a word to one each other.

The next morning I left the mop bucket outside his cell door, hoping he would trip up on it as he came out. 'Who the fuck left this here?', I can hear him shouting. 'What cunt put this here?'

I lose it completely and dive out onto the landing.

'Why don't you shut up, you wanker.' I'm telling him, not asking.

He flies into me and we fall on the floor in a wrestle. A couple of other cons manage to pull us apart, but as soon as he is upright he comes at me again. I manage to ensure that he runs straight on to two lovely shots to his jaw. Crack, crack. His knees bend, but instead of keeling over he lurches forward and grabs me around the neck with both hands as he falls. He's a big guy, and his fingers are coiled around my throat like fat old snakes. He's choking the life out of me and I know I am in trouble. My head feels like it will explode and I cannot breathe. When they show people being strangled in films or on the telly, it looks almost pleasant, like the victim is a bit shocked at first and then just falls off to sleep. But believe me it must be the worst way to die. In desperation I shove my hand between his legs and find his scrotum. Instead of crushing his bollocks, I try to rip his ballbag clean off. I literally try to tear it from his body, and this soon makes him loosen his grip on my neck. Somehow we separate, both shocked at what we have just tried to do to each other, and then retreat back into our cells before the screws appear.

At this time, I had a job on the outside. I was working at the disabled college in Leatherhead, Surrey three or four days a week and I loved it. The work was rewarding and fun and when I was there the days literally flew by. At the end of the day I travelled back to the prison and waited outside to be let back in. Strange, isn't it? Knocking on the gates of a nick and asking to be let in.

One afternoon, waiting outside these big gates was my friend with the sore nuts. I saw him looking at me as I approached and thought, here we go again. I tensed myself, ready to steam straight into him and finish the job once and for all.

'Can I have a word, Jim?' The tone of his voice was friendly, but he could be trying to put me off my guard. I stopped a couple of yards in front of him. 'Look, Jim, what happened the other day. We've both got a lot to lose. It was over nothing. Can we forget it?'

'Forget what?' I grinned. 'Don't know what you're talking about.' He smiled back and we shook hands and remained friendly for the rest of our sentences.

They were a good bunch in Send, and I made some nice friends. Among them was Ronnie Knight, who had come back from Spain to face the music over his alleged role in the famous Brinks Mat robbery. He was a cheerful, funny and wise fella, who got the respect of the other inmates without trying. After we were both released, he organised a party for his friends on the outside and his mates from Send. It was held in a pub in Kent and Ronnie had put on a big spread. He even sent a pony and trap to pick us up from a nearby pub and bring us to the right place. Me and Skunk went, and some other friends of Ronnie and former mates of mine from Send were there too, including Frankie Sims, Bob the Breaker, Bobby Green and Johnny Lloyd. I had taken my girls to the do and they were thrilled to have their photograph taken with the man that used to be married to that lady from *EastEnders*.

Coming out, though, I was bitter. Bitter at how the police had pursued me the way they did. But I had to put it out of my mind. Getting wound up only lands you in more trouble, and I was determined to live my life quietly and peacefully.

Cousin Joe and some other good mates took me on holiday to Benidorm when I came out. The first time I had been abroad was when I went to Tenerife with my friend Dean Boardman a couple of years earlier. I was absolutely terrified of flying, and had to get some pills from the doctor beforehand to calm my nerves. I was meant to be a traveller, but air travel obviously wasn't in the story! I keep hearing about these groups of travellers causing havoc on planes. Well, I don't know how they manage it. Me, I'm rooted to my seat gripping the arms, muscles all tense until we land. But once we arrive I love every minute of it.

In Benidorm with Joe and the boys, I had a great time. One night, whilst we queued for taxis after a late-night disco, a group of drunken, tanned English boys staggered up and jumped the queue. 'There's a queue here, mate,' I pointed out. One of them looked me up and down. He was in his early twenties, I'd guess.

'Is there, mate?' he answered, sarcastically. 'Best get behind me then.'

I looked over at Joe, and Joe looked over at me. We both slowly shook our heads and let the boys jump in the next cab.

I'm still roofing and doing odd jobs here and there. I'm careful now. Paranoid even. Maybe if I do jobs for nothing I'll be safe. I'll probably get nicked even then, for being too cheap.

This book has got me thinking about my life and, except for the sad slaying of my father, I would honestly not change a thing. It has been a good life. I've met and known some wonderful people, experienced some fantastic highs and lows, and it has been exciting and fun, though I've done wrong and I've been wronged. I would like to have been a professional boxing champion like Johnny Frankham, but at least one of our own made it pro, and I did okay as a bare-knuckle man.

I have no hang-ups or guilt about my past. I fought for honour on the whole. I can't understand why anyone would fight purely for fun or when their opponent isn't more or less equally matched, or both parties are up for it. Take football hooligans. What is that all about? Grown men running around in gangs, kicking each other senseless. Knifing people who have done nothing to them or their families – people they have never seen before and will never see again. That's beyond me. And it's not as if they're all going through their teenage or young-man aggressive phase. I've met some of these blokes who are middle-aged, overweight men in their forties.

---

I'm blessed with Wally, Mum and my sisters. I've got Lydia and the kids. I still go over to Dad's grave in Hanwell and sit and look at his picture on the stone. Then I'll tell him what's been happening. I've told him I'm doing a book. That would have confused him, not being able to read and write and all that. I've got everything I need and I've got some lovely, lovely memories.

I don't fight no more. I'm long retired. I'm 42 years of age, and sensible enough to know that my day has long gone. There are some good, young bare-knuckle fighters around and I know I couldn't compete. Wouldn't want to. I'm a family man, minding my own business.

Like most gypsies, I work to live – not live to work. That is one of the real differences between gorgers and travellers. Gorgers see work as one of the most important things in life. Very often it is how they judge others, and what they are judged by. But for us, work is only a means to an end. We are not work-shy, we just can't see the point in doing more than we need to. Living is the most important thing. Being with your family and friends. Because work isn't real – people, your loved ones, are.

There is nothing I like more than to come home from a hard day's work and shower, then take my chair out to the green outside the house and sit and ponder. I live near the airport and the planes come over the fields opposite the house, fields like the ones we parked up on when I was a boy. We don't even notice the planes now as they cast a huge shadow over the green fields and drown out the birds singing and the wind blowing. The modern and the old world co-existing.

Sometimes at night I think the house is moving and lights are flashing past the window, but I'm only dreaming that I'm on the road with Dad singing to himself, or humming along to his favourite Dean Martin songs in the cab, as he drives us through one county into another in the dead of the night. And then I wake up and have my own little wide-awake dream. The one where I march happily down to the bookie's and pick up my winnings because my Jimmy Dean has won his first boxing title.

## EPILOGUE

# A DAY AT THE RACES

**'HOW YA DOING, BRUV?'** It was Jimmy on the line and he was asking how the book was going, how I was doing and how the other Martin (Martin Knight) was doing. Did we want to join him, Wally and a few other pals at Goodwood on Saturday for a day's racing? Since we had first met some five months ago at the Runnymede Hotel to discuss this project, a real friendship had developed between us.

That first day we made polite but cautious conversation as we sounded one another out and weighed each other up. Johnny Bloomfield, the boxing trainer, set up the meeting, and Jimmy brought along his Cousin Joe. Jimmy didn't say a lot that day. He left that to Joe, who worked us over like a tactical boxer with a question here and a question there. Why do you want to do a book about Jimmy? What do you think of gypsies? Why would anyone want to read it? How many will it sell? What else have we done? And so on.

By the time we'd met again they had checked our credentials. Joe visited someone in prison who knew me from my football days and as Joe said, 'He gave you a good name.' Many of Jim's family still live in the same area where the other Martin was raised, and they were assured he was known locally and wasn't some sort of journalist or something, about to sell them down the river.

Soon we got down to business, and slowly Jim began to reveal himself. At his house I always received a warm welcome from Lydia, his wife, and the kids. When I turned up each week to gather information and tape conversations with Jim and the rest of the cast, his girls were constantly crowding around my car as I arrived, firing questions at me, checking my knowledge of the Romany culture.

'What do chokkas mean, Martin?'

'Where's the drag, Martin?'

Towards the end, they were rarely able to catch me out. Those sessions were great fun, although sometimes I'd get home and play the tape and find it was totally unintelligible as Wally and Joe bantered with one another whilst Johnny Frankham told a story to Martin. Only now and then did you hear Jim, who would wait patiently for a lull in the cacophony to answer a question I had put to him earlier.

Jim didn't lay down many rules as to where we could and couldn't go. He insisted from the start that if he said something was true, and it was, then it could go in the book. Indeed, there were times when we suggested to him that certain episodes should remain in his memory. 'Up to you boys, but it's true,' he would shrug.

Even when we discussed things that could be uncomfortable for Jim, such as his father's murder, or his prison sentences, or the common perception of gypsies, he remained open, frank and fair-minded in his opinions. It was the respect he was held in generally as a prizefighter that had prompted us to seek him out, but soon we respected him for the decent, intelligent human being that he is.

Joe Smith, Billy Smith and their respective wives and children, came down to my house for the day we did one chapter on Joe's eventful life: bare-knuckle fighter turned professional golfer. That day was one of those I will treasure among the many meets we had. Another was the day they took me to a caravan site, their natural environment, and sparred with each other for my benefit. Jim and Wally, Wally and Joe, Jim and Joe. With gloves and without gloves. Brothers and cousins drawing friendly blood from one another in the most natural way. I was made so welcome.

The second time on the site I had a professional photographer in tow, who was on edge, to say the least. But after countless cups of tea and a couple of hours, he was on relaxed, first-name terms with everyone. As we left, he said incredulously: 'They're really nice people. My opinion of gypsies was way off the mark.' Another convert.

By the time Jim rang to invite us to go racing with them, I was sorry that the book was coming to an end. I made some very good friends, learned more than I could ever have imagined and, above all, had a lot of fun. 'Of course, Jim, we'd love to come to Goodwood.'

Martin and I met Jimmy at the top of the hill by the entrance to the main stand. It was a perfect, sunny Goodwood afternoon. Jimmy ambled up with his brother Wally, his brother-in-law George and his good friends, Skunk and Toucher. They were all casually but smartly dressed. We picked up some tickets from Tweedy the tout and went inside and found a beer tent with just enough elbow-room at the bar to squeeze in. Wally, Toucher and George pooled their resources and decide to bet as a team, and Jimmy and Martin did the same.

The pints kept coming and we stood around soaking up the atmosphere. It's not Epsom and it's not Ascot. It's Goodwood, with a character all of its own. It doesn't revolve around the ruling classes showing off as at Ascot, or the working class at play at Epsom. It's more like all the English village folk have got together for one big picnic on the rolling downs. There's still plenty of women around, Harvey Nicked to the eyeballs, but they are desirable, attainable even, not like the stuck-up old boilers parading around at Ascot. Mutton dressed as peacock.

In between nipping out to the course to place bets, various members of the travelling clans join our company intermittently: Johnny and Sam Frankham looking like identical twins with three and a half ears between them, and the Chatfields, to name a few.

We all managed to get through the first three races without drawing a penny from the bookmakers between us. I heard Jim say to Martin that if he wants to go on his own, not to be shy, just say so, but Martin said he'd started so he'd finish. Wally's answer to his poor run of luck, it seemed, was to up the ante and huge rolls of notes appeared from various pockets for each race.

Finally, everyone had a draw on the favourite in the fourth race, but it started at even money and nicked back only a fraction of what had been lost. Then Jimmy and Martin have a 13–2 winner and they are in the money. Jimmy had a couple of hundred at least on it.

By the time of the last race, everyone was too weary or perhaps too drunk to watch the actual race. But Wally, Skunk and George pooled the last of their money to try and come out with something, and Jimmy loosened up all his winnings and laid it on the favourite. 'Aren't you going to keep some back?' I asked.

'In for a penny in for a pound,' he smiled.

'But I thought you weren't a gambling man?'

'I'm not, but I am today. Look, Martin, the weather's good, the company is good. Money's for spending, not keeping in your pocket.'

The race is off and everyone crowds around the little screen in the tent. Men and ladies alike are shouting their own nag home.

'Go on, my son!'

'Get in there, my beauty!'

The shouting becomes louder as the race nears its climax. Then it's all over – an outsider has won. Besides the one or two who scuttled off to collect their winnings, the shouts of encouragement quickly turned to recriminations. 'Two-bob wanker.'

'Wants fucking shooting.'

Then came the ritualistic screwing up of the betting cards and casting them to the floor. Jim, though, didn't bat an eyelid when the favourite failed to produce, although he had lost at least £500. He was pleased when Martin pushed £80 into his hand that he had won for them both, when he had decided to back his own choice in the race as well as their joint bet.

With the racing over, the crowds bustled out of the course and swept across the Downs to their parked cars, minibuses and coaches, but we stayed in the beer tent with the others who knew Goodwood and knew that no one would be going anywhere for at least an hour. It was mainly travellers now in the tent and they all seemed to know one another. I guess their fathers, grandfathers and great-grandfathers had done the same before them at every Goodwood meeting, well back into the last century.

As if to underline this feeling of tradition, one gypsy man burst into song and the tent fell silent. It was a crooning number, Frank Sinatra or Tony Bennett or someone. Then, to my surprise, Jim himself began to sing. I thought he was mucking about at first as he locked eyes with me and sung in a strong cowboy accent the story of the horse they called the brute and the man who tamed it in his little cotton suit. He could sing too, and when he had finished the country and western number a round of applause went up inside and outside the tent.

It was the next song that fascinated me, though. Again, Jim sang it with a pronounced country and western twang, but it was about gypsies, and particularly characters I had heard them talk of, some mentioned in the book. I managed to pick up only some of the words:

I like a Transit,
Don't mind a Datsun
As long as it is a running boy
That's good enough for me.

I shot down out of Horsmenden
Shot across the green
Then I see old caller boy
We had to check 'em down
I shot out of Horsmenden
And shot right up the hill.

I like a Transit,
Don't mind a Datsun
As long as it is a running boy
That's good enough for me.

I pulled up outside the Bull
And this is who I see

I see old Frank Mosey
Jasper and his crew
Old Jim was standing against the door
Blowing his mouth organ.

Little Evie was a dancing boy
Up and down the floor
Old Rymer walked up to the bar
With his cauliflower ear
The landlord says, 'I'm sorry, Jack
There's no more beer served here.'

I like a transit,
Don't mind a Datsun
As long as it is a running boy
That's good enough for me.

It was obvious Jim hadn't just made the song up. The words flowed, verse after verse, and a good deal of the people in the tent knew it too. Jim told me that the song was called 'You've Got Some Old Motors' and was written by a man called Ambrose Smith. He said that a tape was pressed of it, and is owned by many travelling people. It fascinated me that although the song wasn't that old (Datsuns not having been around in this country much before 1970), it was so well known but has probably never been written down before. Like most things in the gypsy culture it was passed around from one another and down from one generation to another. It is also firmly tongue in cheek, dealing with travellers and their experiences with clapped-out cars, battle-scarred faces and difficulties over getting served at licensed premises.

Finally, the contract caterers were making themselves busy around us, wanting us to leave but dubious about asking. Apparently, the next port of call was to be the Jarvis Hotel, just outside of Chichester, so we set off to find Skunk's old motor (not a Datsun) among the Mercs, the MGBs and the BMWs still parked on the Downs.

Jim's wife, Lydia, had prepared some food for us earlier and, using Skunk's open boot as a kitchen table, we tucked in, still waiting for the traffic to clear. At this point, our old friend Charlie turned up. It's always nice to see Charlie. 'I didn't know book people got up to this sort of thing,' commented Toucher.

Finally, we piled into Skunk's car. He was stone-cold sober, having been teetotal for some years now, and rattled off to the hotel.

On arrival, we weren't sure we had the right place. It seemed a bit posh, but a head popped out from behind a velvet curtain and waved us into a bar or function room area. Inside, you could be forgiven for thinking it was the annual bash for a city merchant bank, as elegant-looking women chatted together and the men, most of them in well-cut suits, stood or sat around the bar area. The atmosphere was jovial but calm and the drink began to flow again. When we heard Jimmy and the others arranging for a minibus to take us all on to Emsworth to another friendly pub for a late drink with the Frankham entourage, Martin and I knew we wouldn't be able to take the pace and decided to duck out.

Jim followed us out into the car park as we awaited our taxi.

'Thanks for coming, boys,' he said.

'No, Jim, it's been great, we've really enjoyed it.'

He hugged us both and Martin exhaled air in relief as he released his grip. 'Do you know the best thing that has come out of doing this book?' he continued.

'What is that, Jim?'

'I've made two good friends.'

'That's a nice thing to say, Jim.'

'No, I mean it. And I also want you to know, I don't care whether the book sells ten copies, 10,000 copies or 100,000 copies. We've done our best. We've had some fun and you've helped me leave my mark. When I'm gone, there will still be something there. Something my children and their children can read.'

Jim grinned as he immediately saw the irony in what he had said. 'I'll have to make sure they go to school and learn to read and write,' he shrugged and returned to the bar.

# APPENDIX

*Text of a speech made by Eli Frankham, a poet and chairman of the National Romany Rights Association. The speech was made when the last Conservative government were still in power. Eli is a member of the large Frankham family, and is related to Johnny and Sam Frankham, both featured in Jimmy's story.*

The catalogue of atrocities perpetrated against gypsies from the mid 1400s through to the present times – endorsed by state and church – is a tragedy that no author could pen, no single mind conceive, and in a civilised world, no people should have to endure.

Traditionally, gypsies in this country have had very little reason to be interested in or concerned with politics. For hundreds of years, they have travelled the country performing menial tasks, taking and often begging whatever employment they could find, fighting the elements, bigotry and mistrust, often being hounded and harassed from county to county by the constabulary pursuing outdated and archaic laws. Very often, may I add, with much more vigour than was necessary. Many a poor gypsy family went hungry for the day due to a well-aimed police regulation boot being aimed at a pot suspended from a kettle iron over an open fire containing the whole day's supply of food for a family.

It is generally accepted that gypsies arrived in Europe around the 14th century. Almost from the time they arrived, right up to the present day, they have been despised and persecuted. No people on earth have a history of persecution and hatred directed at them for such a prolonged period of time and for no reason. Tell me one war which the gypsies started, tell me one land they tried to occupy by force, tell me one monarch they tried to dethrone, tell me one crime against humanity they have committed.

Is it through lack of understanding, jealousy or fear? True, their manners and customs must have seemed strange; their nomadic way of life must have been at variance with the conventions of settled societies. Fear, though, is often triggered by fascination. Countless painters, musicians and writers have had their imaginations stirred, and some of the public their heads turned, by romantic notions about gypsy weddings and blood brotherhood, scenes of passion to the sound of violins, moonlight, mystery, fortune telling and secret powers. Then there is the disenchanted view of the landowners and gamekeepers who find their coverts raided and their land fouled and littered (often may I say by non-gypsy travellers).

Somewhere between these two extremes the gypsies exist. A people who, in the course of their history, have preserved and sometimes acquired beliefs, customs and traditions which are paralleled in many cultures. A people whose history is preserved in oral traditions and legends, for, being nomadic, the gypsies have not left behind archaeological evidence of settlement or cultivation, and because of their history of cultivation, and their history of illiteracy, no written documentation of any note.

But other documentation is available in various archives, and this much is known; by 1471 the first anti-gypsy laws had been passed in Lucerne, and by 1637 similar laws had spread through Brandenburg, Spain, Germany, Holland, Portugal, England, Denmark, France, Flanders, Scotland, Bohemia, Poland, Lithuania and Sweden. The whole of Europe was encompassed.

The punishment that these laws demanded was varied and vicious. Flogging, torture, branding, mutilation, hanging, shooting, being hunted like animals for sport, bounties being put on their heads and hunted as vermin, the list is endless and the misery incalculable. In England in 1554, Queen Elizabeth I imposed the death penalty, not only for the crime of being a gypsy, but also for anyone in their fellowship or company. Gypsy liaison officers were a scarce commodity in those days.

Scotland continued to enforce such legislation right through to the 18th century and, indeed, much Scottish anti-gypsy law was still on the statute book up to 1906.

In 1994, a Conservative government in England was still passing anti-gypsy law, threatening to destroy homes, confiscate property, split up families, provoke needless confrontations and traumatise innocent children caught up in the middle of it all. There's a stark similarity to Germany in the late 1930s and early 1940s, don't you think? And 1994 was the Conservative government's 'Year of the Family'. This is a government more dedicated to legalising the buggering of 16-year-old boys than providing conditions for travellers to live within the law, following the only way of life they and their ancestors have known.

We now have ethnic cleansing by legislation – far more subtle and far more dangerous than ethnic cleansing by violence. That can be fought against, you can see your enemy, fight your enemy, crush your enemy. There is no such recourse with cleansing by legislation. Unjust laws are something different. You may despise them, you may disobey them, you may argue against them, but you cannot destroy them, cannot crush them. They are always there and your way of life is always in peril, constantly under threat.

Once on the statute books, history has shown such laws will not readily be repealed. If anything, they will be reinforced by reforms. Too many species on this planet have become extinct, and too many species today are endangered – are the gypsies now to be added to the list? Why? In this country – and quite rightly too – there are laws to protect the birds of the air, the flowers of the field and the majority of our natural wildlife, with penalties ranging from heavy fines to imprisonment – yet there is not one law to protect the gypsy.

British justice, we are told, is the envy of the world. The British sense of fair play is legendary; the British will lay down their lives in the defence of the underprivileged and oppressed. How and where these myths originated is a mystery. How they have lasted and endured is an even greater mystery.

The British Empire was one of the greatest the world has ever known. It was taken by the sword and held down by oppression and exploitation. How many poor souls perished through torture, slavery and trying to defend his or her freedom is anybody's guess. Millions would be a conservative estimate. These atrocities were not only confined to foreign shores either – the peasants' revolt of 1341, led by Wat Tyler, Richard Kett and John Ball against the closing of common lands to the common people – does that ring a bell?

And the opposition to a poll tax (do I hear another bell ringing?) which was brutally and savagely put down by the Earl of Warwick, later elevated to the Duke of Northumberland, who it is said only thought of money and power (another bell rings). His accomplice was Humphrey Arundel of Cornwall and Devon, whose main claim to fame was that he was a powerful landowner who denied the ancient common rights to his tenants.

The Tolpuddle Martyrs were deported for standing up for their rights. The Jarrow marchers and, more recently, the workers at GCHQ, Cheltenham, and the miners have all had their rights denied them in this free and democratic country.

English history is littered with such instances. In fact, it is almost entirely made up of them; oppression and subservience go hand in hand, taking away the citizens' rights to any land they occupied when it suited them.

However, to get to the gypsies, the 1968 Caravan Act gave us cause to believe that at long last our struggle for recognition was being acknowledged, progress was being made and our children would be educated, would receive proper health care and we would be accepted by society. In short, we would be treated like human beings. How short-lived that jubilation proved to be, how empty those promises turned out, how typical of that government's hypocrisy.

The wheel has turned full circle since, and the wrath of the state is being vented upon the gypsy population again, with laws exhibiting not just a dislike for the underprivileged and despised but also portraying a physical expression of hatred. Laws are being wheedled through parliament by chicanery and deception, trickery and guile, devoid of democracy, devoid of compassion and devoid of shame. A purely social problem is given pride of place in a Criminal Justice Bill. What an indictment of British democracy!

I stated earlier that politics played no part in the gypsies' lives. That is rapidly changing. The gypsy is beginning to realise that it is not the man in the street, not the man in the blue uniform, that is his enemy. The pinstriped politicians stomping through the corridors of Whitehall in jackboot fashion, calling each other honourable and not knowing the meaning of the word – they are his true enemy. It is ironic that the laws now being framed, which this government claims are for the benefit of the gypsies, are so Machiavellian in their structure. Misleading information oozes from this government like pus from an ulcer, whilst beneath the skin the problem festers untreated.

Certain segments of society have always from time to time had Draconian laws aimed at them, resulting in bloodshed, misery and torment. Witches, 'heretics' and Jews spring readily to mind. They all have one thing in common: the laws are now repealed and the persecution is a thing of the past. The gypsies stand alone, unique as the only segment of society whereby such laws have not been repealed. In fact, today, the laws are being strengthened and made even more insidious. Leave or be hounded to death – every country in Europe has attempted this legislation at least once against the gypsies. Britain is now falling in line with that maxim once again.

Let us ponder here for a moment on what the problem really is. It is a government-induced situation, induced deliberately, mischievously, and with malice. They are intent on destroying the nomadic way of life. Give us back our traditional stopping places. Give us back our freedom; our freedom to travel without let or hindrance. Set aside basic sites, which allow us to follow our way of life without committing trespass. If a traveller wishes to purchase a piece of land and settle, for God's sake why not encourage him? As the law stands, you do not want him to settle (at least where he wants to be) and you do not want him to travel. What do you want? The answer is inescapable: you do not want gypsies anywhere, at any cost.

The popular concept of a gypsy camp is a roadside settlement, littered and fouled, with no sanitation or refuse disposal – filth and squalor unbridled. Every one of you here can imagine it in your mind's eye, I am sure. The next part takes a bit more concentration. Imagine one of your council estates in the middle of town, with its high concentration of children and household pets such as cats and dogs. Now imagine the water supply being disconnected permanently. No more water on tap. No more hot baths. No more showers. No more toilets being flushed. Now imagine the estate road being torn up and the refuse service being abolished. You now have no road, no water and your own litter is in the house and in your garden. After four to five days, the bins are overflowing and the cats and dogs are foraging amongst it. The toilet is still not getting flushed weeks later – can you imagine it? Imagine it! You can almost smell it. After six months of council or private house tenants living like this, it would be the gypsies down the road complaining to the health authorities about the health hazards, the squalor and the filth lowering the tone of their surroundings.

I say to you, any encampment of travellers without the basic facilities of water, sanitary and refuse disposal is an indictment of the local authorities, who should by law be obliged to supply these minimal services which every householder takes for granted and all too willingly denies to others.

The attempts by the government and some local authorities to wriggle out of their duty by promoting Romanies and marginalising the so-called tinkers, didicois and New Age travellers is a scapegoat mechanism, used by society against the gypsies and by the gypsies against each other. It is government propaganda, aggravating the situation not addressing it. If the needs of nomadic people are ever to be addressed, the definition must be simplified, not made even more complicated. All the rubbish being talked about New Age travellers is meaningless rhetoric, aimed at stirring up discontent. The problem should have been solved before the New Age travellers ever appeared on the scene.

Much has been made about how much has been spent on sites: £78 million has been quoted. That represents about £3 million a year for the duration of the Caravan Act. The drinks bill for government ministers last year was £15 million. That gives some idea of the seriousness with which they have tackled the issue of site provision.

In democratic Britain there are only two legal reasons for subjecting a person to restraint: one is that he is accused of an offence and must be brought before a court of law, and the other is that he has been convicted of an offence and is undergoing punishment. A man may not have his liberty of movement interfered with, except as a suspected or actual criminal. Where does that leave the gypsy? A criminal by birth. A criminal by virtue of having no legal and lawful sites to move onto. His liberty of movement denied him. An exile in his homeland. This is Britain now, a land that millions have died for to preserve us from tyranny and oppression. Would their sacrifice have been so willing if they could see their beloved country as it is today?

Corruption permeates through sport, politics and law. The unaccountability of the ruling class, the persecution of the working class and the hatred of the underclass is more obvious, not less. The impotence of the Church in combating our moral decline is shocking, as is the despair that is choking the life out of young and old. Helplessness hangs like a dense fog over all the land.

When Moses came down from Mount Sinai, God had given him ten laws – ten laws which our Creator considered sufficient for men and women to live in peace and harmony if he heeded them. Today, we have 10,000 laws for each of the ten – all man-made. But now we have more starvation, more misery, more wars, more envy, more hatred, more greed, more murder, more rape, more injustice and more social discontent than at any other time in our history.

Surely there is a moral in there somewhere? Maybe we need only one law, a law that is constant, that needs no amendments, no sub-clauses, no reforming.

That law is: live and let live.

I thank you.

**Eli Frankham, 1994**

# FURTHER READING

*Bareknuckles: A Social History of Prize-Fighting*, Dennis Brailsford, Lutterworth Press, 1988

*Fairfield Folk: A History of the British Fairground and its People*, Frances Brown, Malvern Publishing Company, 1986

*Gypsies: An Illustrated History*, Jean-Pierre Liegeois, Al Saqi Books, 1986

*Jem Mace: His Life Story Told By Himself*, Peter McInnes, Caestus Books, 1998

*Moving On: The Gypsies and Travellers of Britain*, Donald Kenrick and Colin Clark, University of Hertfordshire Press, 1995

*People of the Road: The Irish Travellers*, Mathias Oppersdorff, Syracuse University Press, 1997

*Stop the Ride I Want tŒ o Get Off*, Dave Courtney, Virgin Books, 1999

*Tales of the Old Gypsies*, Jennifer Davies, David & Charles, 1999